Printing Statement:

Due to the very old age and scarcity of this book,
many of the pages may be hard to read due to the
blurring of the original text, possible missing pages,
missing text, dark backgrounds and other issues
beyond our control.

Because this is such an important and rare work, we
believe it is best to reproduce this book regardless of
its original condition.

Thank you for your understanding.

comprehensive American research, and to add
a tiny mite toward lifting its efficiency through
indicating its charm, its national worth at this
time, the educational requirements to those
new in the field, and in pointing out the reasons
for loss in efficiency through misconceptions,
intense duplication work, and the many snares
and pitfalls awaiting the unwary inventor.
Major General William M. Black, Chief of
Engineers, United States Army, pointed out
that the Government in Washington was simply
deluged with suggestions and so-called inventions from all over the country for the winning
of the war.

The records show that about 98 per cent of
all the inventions examined were declared to
be without military value and that time and
labor have been thrown away by men eager to
help, but entirely ignorant of the history and
conditions of warfare.

It is also pointed out that the Naval Consulting Board had sixty thousand inventions submitted with but substantially the same low
average of practical merit. The same inefficiency occurs in times of peace through tens of
thousands of men working upon problems, in
the history and conditions of which they are
equally ignorant, and moreover they are frequently working upon problems they are not
educationally equipped to develop.

It is now in the field of peace research that we should emphasize efficiency.

Dr. W. R. Whitney, a famous American research chemist, states:

" We are generally superficial. The interesting lives of a few exceptionally able American inventors have led us to overprize engineering short cuts. We are patenting inventions at the rate of nearly fifty thousand a year, but very few Americans are advancing the sciences at all."

Dr. J. S. Ames, an equally famous physicist, writes:

" One illustration of this may suffice; one government board, with whose activity I am familiar, has had submitted to it in the course of the year 16,000 projects and devices, proposed by so-called inventors; of these only five had sufficient value to deserve encouragement. I have nothing but admiration for those 15,995 men, whose disappointment must have been keen. Most of them were more than willing to give their inventions freely to the government. The point I wish to emphasize is that the ability and knowledge required in waging this war successfully are not those possessed by any body of men except those with a profound knowledge of science and of scientific method. The problems are too complicated. It is true that with the help of trained technical men we will get better engines, better explosives, better guns; and for these we should be truly grateful to our much-boasted American genius. But, consider a problem like this: To devise a light signal, which can be used by day or by night, and which will be absolutely invisible to the enemy. Who can solve that? The answer is obvious: Only a physicist."

I shall write much in the first person at the risk of being criticised as egotistical, but in the interest of directness, for first-hand experiences are usually more readable. I am moreover enabled, by writing in this vein, to reflect in many instances the views and comments of the many brilliant men of Dr. Whitney's and Dr. Ames' calibre with whom I have come in contact or with whom I have been associated in my war work in the Council of National Defense, The National Research Council, the specialists in the Army and Navy, the chemists, physicists, metallurgists and engineers at the Bureau of Mines Experiment Station, and the War Experiment Station at the American University, together with the technical staffs of the French, British and Italian High Commissions, and I shall quote freely from the writings of distinguished scientists and scholars where they treat of the subjects under discussion.

It is hoped by this method that some economic good may be brought about by showing how many students and inventors are today working hopelessly and how many fall into the hands of inferior profit-taking patent attorneys who advertise in sensational ways, and how weeks and months, and sometimes years could be saved and hundreds and often thousands of dollars could be conserved, if the research workers and inventors were only honestly and unselfishly told something of the prior art. But we have too large a number of unconscientious attorneys who hourly add many worthless patents to the thousands of like kind already in existence.

With our factories, on the other hand, another kind of waste and inefficiency is apparent. Too many are without research laboratories or research affiliations, for today it is but an antique policy to attempt to maintain a supremacy either by efforts to keep processes or methods of manufacture secret, or by relying upon a patent. A live competitor with experimental and research facilities will sooner or later discover other, and often superior, ways of accomplishing the same ends. To put the situation in other words, no method of manufacture or process or art can live for long these days, which is not advancing scientifically.

And last, but by no means least, is the important subject, how to equip for and how to carry on research work. Even wise heads trained for the theme and with definite ideas

with the most exquisitely made and elaborate tools, and all with an equally happy absorption.

From the bone and stone implements to the polished lenses, the delicate balances, the jeweled meters, the ponderous hammers and mighty engines, the research worker and inventor forges on in war time and in peace with a natural instinct and with a contented spirit.

Of Ericson, the inventor of the monitor, which revolutionized naval warfare, we read that " he was never so happy as when engaged with his drawing. . . . As a draughtsman he had no rival, past or present, and the outlines of new devices grew upon the paper as if by magic."

And in connection with war and instrumental contrivance, Dr. Whitney says, " From the military expert to the anthropologist, thinking men recognize that for over one hundred thousand years war has been almost continuous on earth. The inventors of chipped flint successfully fought those inferiors who had not *experimented* with flint"; and continuing, Dr. Whitney very aptly points out that " the fundamentals were always the same. A 42 cm. gun is only a better flint, trinitrotoluol is only a more modern sling."

From a study of psychological literature in quest of a better understanding of the term " instinct," we find it characterized by Professor William James, the great psychologist, as follows:

" They (the instincts) are the functional correlatives of structure. The nervous system is, to a great extent, a preorganized bundle of such reactions. Every instinct is an impulse. Whether we call such impulses as blushing, sneezing, coughing, smelling, or dodging, or keeping time to music, instincts or not, it is a mere question of terminology. The process is the same throughout."

And so with the instinct of workmanship, the mainspring, or natural driving force which impelled Ericson and thousands of others to design and construct, and which will ever continue to act in the march of progress. We might list some of the other human instincts, and because of the economic value to the nation, place the instinct of workmanship at the top, followed by the instinct of self-preservation, of play, adventure, flight, sex, pugnacity, imitation, hunting, curiosity, the chase; of gambling, sympathy, devotion, domination, drama, migration, expression, ownership, religion, morality, modesty, aestheticism, collecting, rhythm, movement, ratiocination, acquisitiveness, depredation.

If we recognize that men are compelled to work by a natural driving force, or instinct of contrivance which fills their hearts, does not efficiency and progress to success, whether of the individual or of the nation, depend upon the educational rudder to direct this driving force? Does not success depend upon a wider knowledge, or the selected fruits of special education? It is of course true that many inventions have been made by men with but little education, and often by men from one field of activity entering another with many of the factors most essential, "a free brain, a clear insight, and fresh enthusiasm." Many inventors are working as much in the dark today as the Hermit Philosophers and Alchemists were, working in the dark and middle ages; and many are as ignorant of the laws of science as King Chata, of the first dynasty, who reigned 4000 B.C., was of medicine, for the following amusing prescription for promoting the growth of hair is taken for example from the art of his time.

Pad of a dog's foot. 1
Fruit of a date palm. 1
Ass's hoof. 1
     Boil together in oil.

Let us set forth another formula here, one of the Alchemists', to show how far they wandered at times in the fields of absurdity. They were seeking here the " Electrum Magicum," a complex metal alloy from which to make tiny mirrors which they believed would enable them to see events of the past and the present, as well as absent friends and enemies. Here is the remarkable formula:

" Take ten parts of pure gold, ten of silver, five of copper, two of tin, two of lead, one part of powdered iron and five of mercury. All these metals must be pure. Now wait for the hour when the planets Saturn and Mercury come into conjunction, and have all your preparations ready for that occasion; have the fire, the crucible, the mercury and the lead ready, so that there will be no delay when the time of the conjunction arrives, for the work must be done during the moments of the conjunction. As soon as this takes place, melt the lead and add the mercury and let it cool. After this has been done, wait for a conjunction of Jupiter with Saturn and Mercury, melt the compound of lead and mercury in a crucible, and in another crucible the tin, and pour the two metals together at the moment of such conjunction. You must now wait until a conjunction of the Sun with either one or both of the above-named planets takes place, and then add the gold to the compound after melting it previously. At a time of the conjunction of the moon with the Sun, Saturn and Mercury, the silver is added likewise, and at a time of the conjunction of Venus with one of the above-named planets the copper is added. Finally, at a time of such a conjunction with Mars, the whole is completed by the addition of the powdered iron. Stir the fluid mass with a dry rod of witch-hazel, and let it cool."

It is interesting to note that all of the above named planitary conjunctions take place in our

solar system in the course of thirteen successive months, and very sad to believe that
thousands of men today are working upon inventions equally hopeless.   In chemistry, in
comparatively recent times, the famous phlogis-
ton theory led men in the wrong direction for
nearly a century, and Kepler's guesses on the
mechanics of the solar system kept astrono-
mers for years in a state of chaos.   But alchemy
has by no means been in vain, for in the search
for the electrum magicum, the fixation of mercury, the elixir of immortal youth, and the art
of transmutation of the metals, many real discoveries were made in the elements, and in
the arts; for example, Brant discovered the
element phosphorous in his alchemist laboratory, and Kunkle discovered the art of making
ruby glass.   The work of the Alchemists is so
voluminous, and in many phases so important,
that The Alchemical Society was founded in
London in 1912, and the following is from its
constitution:

"The objects of the society shall be the study
of the works and theories of the Alchemists in all
their aspects, philosophical, historical, and scientific, and of matters relating thereto."

Discovery and invention are very closely
allied, and it should be appreciated that they
mutually contribute toward each other's advancement; and that a discovery in the more

scholarly sense goes farther than the revelation of a new fact, or the framing of a new law, applicable to the art in which the research worker happens to be engaged, in that it has a wide cultural aspect as a contribution to the world's storehouse of human knowledge. To enter into the sovereignty of nature, to appreciate the great achievements already made, by a full comprehension of the separate steps taken, by a knowledge of the reverse of the fabric, so to speak, brings, next to actual discovery, great happiness to the true inventor's heart.

In the course of our work we come into contact with all types engaged in research, from the careless non-systematic fellow, but with a certain valor of ignorance, who is content if he succeeds, with "guessing at half and multiplying by two," all the way up the line to the painstaking experimenter, or mathematical worker.

We have experiences with the arrogant and overconfident type, wrapped up in his own conceit, and with the belligerent and suspicious type, whose intellectual equipment is so light that he cannot appreciate wherein he is inferior to a Faraday, a Henry, or a Newton.

It is always amusing to think of this class of individuals in connection with the lines of Wordsworth on Newton's statue at Cambridge University in England.

" The marble index of a mind forever
  Wandering through strange fields of thought
    alone."

We also come in contact with the charming and modest type of real genius, well equipped and industriously seeking for greater knowledge.

Newton once said that he made his discoveries by " intending " his mind on the subjects, and upon another occasion he said, " By always thinking about them," but this should not discourage nor detract from the fact that men of far less mental caliber have accomplished great things because of the pure passion of research which animated them. And after discounting our rather boastful spirit, it may be pointed out that we have much of this wonderful material in America. James Bryce, former Ambassador from Great Britain to the United States, and one of our country's keenest and ablest critics, said that we possess "enthusiasm for anything that may be called genius, and an ever readiness to discover it," and exercise of creative imagination often leads to strokes of genius, and the term " genius " is often given to those believed to possess superior intellectual power. Dr. Channing said that " genius is not a creator, in the sense of fancying or feigning what does not exist: *its distinction is, to discern more of Truth than ordinary minds.*" Perhaps the term "ingenuity" may be taken as a lower form of genius, which upon development grows into the greater power.

An excellent illustration of the difference between *ingenuity* and *genius* is found in the comparison of Kepler and Newton. Kepler advanced several highly ingenuous hypotheses, but it remained for Newton's constructive genius to give the true insight into the facts of the solar system and its mechanics.

Bacon, according to Huxley, had the theory that man could by direct design work for definite goals on the principle that researches " were a kind of mining operation and only required well-directed picks and shovels." I believe that this attitude is perfectly sound, but that the chances of success depend upon the talent in directing the picks. In mining, men do not as a rule go out and dig, but are guided by geologists and mining engineers. In the field of invention and research, we may to advantage at times call in the services of the research engineer, and it very often happens, when we miss the definite object sought, that we by accident uncover something equally valuable and unheard of.

This method of working for definite " fruits " has been styled " Baconian induction," which advocates the " anticipating of nature," which often depends upon the inventing of working hypotheses.

A detective, in unraveling a mystery, works deductively by a close examination of the clues and facts, and where these are meager or missing, he projects an invented working hypothesis, or a whole series of working hypotheses, and then he " intends " his mind, and the minds of his associates upon possible solutions. Many a hiding culprit, like an elusive fact in nature, has been uncovered by this method of investigation. What theory projects in science and research, the theorist essays to substantiate by experiment. He tries through practical methods to secure experimental evidence in support of his projected theories. The demonstrative experiment is therefore the step intermediate between theory and practice, the linking medium which causes them to go hand in hand. Some experiments are unfortunately very expensive of execution, and ways and means must be found to subject a promising theory to experimental demonstration. This is only a part of research and inventive engineering, so necessary if the work is to reap any practical success. Some minds are especially brilliant in the art of promoting research by the faculty of asking pertinent and adroit questions which stimulate inquiry, but often here the talent ceases, the type of mind being unsuited to the engineering phase of actually carrying out the work. The diagnos-

tician in medicine and surgery points out the
conditions, but leaves the next step to the
prescribing physician or the operating surgeon.
The old-fashioned general practitioner used to
undertake the entire thing, sometimes with
failure, and often with brilliant success.   The
modern research laboratory with its elaborate
equipment contains general practitioners and
specialists also, and holds all the romance
man's heart could desire.   In a well-equipped
experimental laboratory and experimental shop
one may as an adventurer enter the forest of
the great unknown as completely as any other
type of adventurous discoverer.

"Every usable drug," says Jordan, "and
every usable instrument is on tap.   A button
brings the investigator all the books of all the
ages, all the records of past experience, carrying knowledge far ahead of his present requirements."   But no single laboratory and its staff
could possibly cover all the requirements of all
problems that are developing daily, and we
must use many equipments and men in different parts of the country selectively.   I believe
that invention and research may be broadly
divided into two schools, one inductive and the
other deductive, and perhaps different types of
minds divide themselves after a fashion into
these two classes.   Let me illustrate, through
the analogy of writing, these two respective

methods in research. Take the case of the
author in literature who wishes to produce a
story, a work of fiction for example. He wishes
to create an interesting, readable book, with an
absorbing plot, — a gem if possible in literature,
one truthful in its setting and atmosphere, in
its coloring and in its historical accuracy and
in the portrayal of the human character. Is
he not an inventor at work? Must he not have
constructive and creative imagination? De-
scriptive of Scott's "lavish imagery," his bi-
ographer writes: "Metaphorical illustrations,
which men born with prose in their souls hunt
for painfully, and find only to murder, were, to
him, the natural and necessary offspring and
playthings of ever-teeming fancy. He could not
write a note to his printer, he could not speak
to himself in his diary, without introducing
them." Is not the artist who seeks more than
mural decoration, also an inventor, as well as
the musical composer? And, of all musicians,
Mozart appears to have had the *inventive* faculty most strongly developed. It has been said
that he could "never draw upon it without
having his draft instantly honored." But to
return to our literary effort. One method is
through inductive writing, based upon profound and broad education, and with a highly
stimulated imagination. The other method
which may be called the deductive method is

where the author with less essential imagination, but with the natural passion to produce
something, and with the love and ability to go
out and study things animate and inanimate,
puts himself in the atmosphere of a quaint
little street or town.   Or perhaps he goes to
the thoroughfares of a great city, with men in
the open, or in the mines, or at sea, to meet
and know the people he describes, to study
their heart's desires and to get the full local
colors of their surroundings and to have a
keen and sympathetic understanding of how
the other fellow lives.   He is the research
author, the deductive writer.   The inductive
author draws upon his accumulated knowledge
and his highly stimulated imagination and
projects the story without leaving his writing
table.   He exercises a constructive imagination
with a mind richly stored with materials.   The
same scheme could be applied to science and
invention, if conditions allowed inventors to go
about more, to learn what has been done and
of what others are doing.   This he can accom-
plish to a large extent by proper reading and
study, if he cannot actually travel, and in this
way avoid fruitless effort, duplication, snares
and pitfalls.   If the inventive type of mind
could be assisted in getting this broader view,
a much higher efficiency in American research
would result.   If a workable plan could be

devised to discover and take a promising genius
out of the drudgery of routine work, and provide for his following his natural bent, the
ultimate service to the nation might be very
great.   Let him be shown high standards, in
order to measure his own efforts, and be
guided in his reading to secure inspiration
from such illustrious names in deductive
research as Joseph Priestly, John Dalton,
Gay-Lussac, Lavoisier, Avogadro, Faraday, Sir
Humphrey Davy, and Joseph Henry.   Clark
Maxwell, on the other hand, the great English
inductive mathematical worker, stands in
sharp contrast, in his methods, to our own
experimental deductive Joseph Henry, who belonged to the experimental school of Avogadro,
whose discovery of the gas laws was one of
the greatest in science.   Avogadro expounded
experimentally and deductively the great fundamental laws of gases in 1811, and handicapped
as he was, with the crudest research tools and
apparatus, he demonstrated that equal volumes
of all gases in like conditions of temperature
and pressure contain an equal number of molecules.   In the light of modern knowledge this
may not be strictly true, but it was a master-
piece of research work, and not fully appreciated until 1840, forty-nine years after he
completed his epoch-making experiments. It was
not until the balance became the ruling instru-

There are, in this connection, at least two methods of classifying men, — by reputation, and according to natural gifts.

The first classification is by reputation and is a misleading one, and the second classification is obviously very difficult of achievement.

A man's success in many fields depends upon opportunities and upon natural power of intellect, and sometimes he must possess both of these factors.

It is where small men become "great" through opportunity alone that it is regrettable.

The saying "The survival of the fittest" has always been a very irritating one to the writer, since many, many cases of the survival of the *unfit* have come under his notice. Since, according to our quotation, "the greatest admirals have gone down in their ships" and the soundest thinking minds have not come to the light of recognition, if in dealing with the subject I take a different point of view from the one of customary praise, one which I believe to be better for the immediate future of our country, I hope that I may not be misunderstood as unsympathetic or in the least unpatriotic.

Professor Simon Newcomb, the preëminent genius of American science, wrote relative to the comparatively few men who have demonstrated the profoundest ability in the field of research:

" It is impressive to think how few men we should have to remove from the earth during the past three centuries to have stopped the advance of our civilization. In the seventeenth century there would have been only Galileo, Newton, and a few contemporaries; in the eighteenth, they could almost have been counted on the fingers; and they have not crowded the nineteenth.

"Even today, almost every great institution for scientific research owes its being to some one man, who, as its founder or regenerator, breathed into it the breath of life. If we think of the human personality as comprehending not merely mind and body, but all that the brain has set in motion, then may the Greenwich Observatory of today be called Airy; that of Pulkowa, Struve; the German Reichsanstalt, Helmholtz; the Smithsonian Institution, Henry; the Harvard Museum of Comparative Zoölogy, Agassiz; the Harvard Observatory, Pickering."

But Professor Newcomb was listing great institutions and their subsequent world influences rather than men perhaps, so under this interpretation, I may, without presumption, add the following names in alphabetical order, as standing for, in many instances, equal brilliance with those supplied: Archimedes, Avogadro, Becquerel, Berthelot, Bessemer, Bell, Brashear, Cavendish, Charles, Coulomb, Crookes, Davy, Dumas, Daguerre, Darwin, Dewar, Dulong, Edison, Ericsson, Faraday, Franklin, Gay-Lussac,

Henry, Joule, Kelvin, Kepler, Langley, Lavoisier,
Le Chatelier, Myer, Mendeleeff, Maxwell,
Morse, Newton, Newcomb, Oersted, Ohm, Pas-
cal, Ptolemy, Pasteur, Priestley, Ramsay, Rayleigh, Thomson, Tesla, Tyndall, Volta, Wheat-
stone.

If more references are made to England,
France, and even to Germany than to America
in the following pages, I shall still ask for the
reader's broader view, his full sportsman's
view, for in books on invention and research
in the past we have rather formed the habit
of emphasizing, if not actually boasting, of
American work, and left as a background the
older, and in many instances the more fundamental foreign achievements.

This national habit among certain classes of
people who believe that we invented everything
in sight, is a bit analogous to the belief among
our more ignorant and over-enthusiastic Americans who claim, and really believe, that we
have just won the world war, practically single-
handed, without fully appreciating the heroic
valor of the Belgians and the French, and that
old England, against which nation stupid school
books have wrought a regrettable prejudice,
went in at the drop of the hat, and that she held
the German battle fleet like a granite wall,
until her merchant marine carried our armies
over-seas to reinforce her seven million men

with her extra equipment in guns and other munitions to spare. Let us be the sportsmen that we are in conceding merit everywhere and ever strive toward higher and higher efficiency at home.

We have expanded from internal and local modes of thinking and acting, into international methods of thought and action, and the successful research worker and inventor should now awaken fully to the broader view by extending his horizon and area of contact as much as possible by the study of contemporary literature and by as much travel as practicable. The sooner the average inventor can abandon ingrowing habits of thought, the more rapid will be his development. There are many able scientific men in America whom the world *should* and *would* know if only they could be relieved from the strain of heavy routine executive work, or be allowed, or forced out from the narrow confines of their own laboratories and shops, and mentally stretch and look about them and compare notes with others.

There is another class who have been accustomed to the praise and applause of immediate friends and misleading admirers in a little community, and who do not appreciate how limited are their horizons, and remain self-satisfied and complacent in the often damaging applause.

I find the average American mechanic usually

trivance and with the use of language as an
instrument of thought with which to record and
transmit his activities. And the mainspring of
the human motor in research is believed to be
a natural instinct, often amounting to a ruling
passion. Let us examine this phenomenon a
little before proceeding farther, to ascertain if
it is not really a strong part of even the lay
reader's equipment. If we grant that most
of us have this propelling power, then the
steering rudder to success only remains to be
provided.

The lower animals possess instinct to even
a higher degree than man, but man's powers of
reason and contrivance more than make up for
this inferiority. It is this instinct of instrument
contrivance, to further his natural love for
workmanship, which, more than any other intellectual activity, places man so far above the
beasts. Among all the instincts with which
man is endowed, psychologists ascribe the highest survival value to the *instinct of industrial
driving force,* and the *instinct of instrumental
contrivance.*

The pine-warbler constructs its nest at the
top of a tall tree without tools, from a natural
instinct which fills its heart, and the true research worker, since the days of the Hermit
Philosophers and Alchemists, fashions his inquiry, sometimes with the simplest, and often

very self-satisfied and conceited, and mainly so from the want of contact with those in broader fields.

Reacting against such a shut-in feeling in a Washington laboratory in 1914, I started just before the war clouds gathered for an inspection trip around the world, with the object of coming into contact with other workers and other laboratories and other experimental shops in order to bring home with me the knowledge of how little I really knew. Then again, things don't stand still and I wished to note the progress on the other side in laboratories, research standards, factories and production methods.

With all the schemes I had invented and improvised, ethically to carry out my purpose, I but succeeded in getting caught in Russia during the mobilization for the world war, and there I recorded many things I did not know before. It had been one of my plans to go into a German factory as a workman, as I had here in America, and luckily for me, I selected other ways and means, and passed through Germany into Russia.

And in connection with applause, I remember very well starting to clap enthusiastically an exquisitely rendered piece of music by a violinist in a restaurant near the Nikolayevski Bridge in Petrograd, when my Russian guide Antonoff pulled the sleeve of my coat, and I found in practice my pet theory. " We do not praise such achievements by applause, sir," he said. — " It is not done in Russia," and he explained that the reason lay in the idea that withholding the applause inspired talent to strive constantly for higher and higher order of merit. It was a bit disconcerting and discomforting undoubtedly to many who strive seriously at the violin, but was it not an improvement over the immoderate applause we so often hear in the vaudeville shows over here after the strumming on banjos or the bellowing of accordions?

The real genius should be less inspired by such easily won applause, and more content in the consciousness of deserving it.

Where do men of genius in the various great activities come from?

Sir Francis Galton selected one hundred Englishmen of well-marked meritorious achievement, and after carefully tracing the origin of each man, found that only four per cent came from the manual laboring classes. My analysis of this poor showing in the laborer is lack of education and mental training of those who work long hours in the shops and factories. I believe the universal introduction of the eight-hour day will go a long way to correct this lack of opportunity for development and I would suggest that such workmen as may have more time under this eight-hour day, spend their leisure or golden hours to better advantage than agitating for a six-hour day, a four-hour day and what not. I would advise their studying some well-established and sound constructive subjects, instead of, especially at this time, being led or coerced by soap-box orators, or selfish labor delegates with no perspective, or by I. W. W. leaders, into dabbling in socialism or any other vague political or so-called economic movement.

Of course I would not expect all workmen who may receive this advice to follow it, but I am confident, from an intimate knowledge of the prodder in sound *well-established* arts and sciences, that if he devotes his time to fighting his way through acquiring knowledge, instead of through hate and dynamite, he will reach a far richer goal in a far shorter time.

M. Odin made a like study of six thousand Frenchmen of eminent attainment, and his alignment with the English experimenter was fairly good, showing a parallel of 9.8 per cent in the production of genius for the laboring classes. Monsieur Odin lists the results of his inquiries as follows:

Nobility............................25 per cent
Government Officials................20 per cent
Liberal Professions.................23 per cent
Bourgeoisie.........................11 per cent
Manual Laborers....................9.8 per cent

This table was so forceful in its lesson that its tabulator exclaimed:

" Genius is in things, not in men."

I am now at work upon an American tabulation, and whereas I have not complete data enough to draw final conclusions for insertion in the present book, I am led to believe that genius among American laborers will show a considerably higher percentage, that intellectual attainment as evidenced in invention and discovery will be more conspicuous than in either England or France.

I think that this may be due, to a considerable extent, to our many moderate-priced and excellent semi-technical magazines, as well as the elaborately illustrated instruction sheets sold by the several correspondence schools. Ultimately, in America, I am very sure with the more thorough education of the children that drift into the great manual laboring classes, that a much higher percentage of laboring men, and women will rise to high positions and even fame.

There is the best of such material here to work upon, especially among the children from farms and little towns who filter through the schools to the factories. At the present time, however, about 90 per cent of American school children stop their studies with the Grammar school.

If their schooling, and the accompanying training of the mind, could be continued for another year or two, there is but little doubt of their ultimate increased chances to rise from the ranks of the laboring classes, a great army whose opportunities and influence in America have already been enormously increased by the fortunes of war.

To develop the intellectual and inventive powers of those who work in the shops, I would recommend constructive study in the sound arts and sciences as already outlined, and *travel*. Do not be prematurely shocked at this last suggestion, for I do not mean that the workman should travel around the world, but that he should travel from one field of activity into another, whereby he may gain an insight into many industries. I would not have made such a suggestion, of course, during the war, for obvious reasons, but I know of no other ways and means for equal development, apart from reading, which are comparable. Let me illustrate specifically. It is quite radical, I am aware, and like the proposing of a new invention, it is likely in some quarters to bring forth the usual jeers of the incredulous. If a man has been engaged in a steel plant for a number of years, let him arrange to work for a month, let us say, in a soap and candle factory; then let him arrange to work for a month in a clock factory, then in a glass works, in an oil-cloth factory, a gas plant, a piano factory, a paper mill, a pyrotechnic factory, on pottery and earthen ware, on musical instruments, on cash registers, on automobiles, etc.; it is not necessary to extend the list further for purposes of illustration. It is true that he could not go from one plant to another and draw the same pay he had been drawing as a result of competency and efficiency, but in the long run he would not be out very much, and if, for the sake of argument, he went to a dozen different factories in a year, counting the matter of reduced wages and railroad fare, he would get a practical working type of education cheap and a stimulus that could not be compared with the expenditure. And this matter of travel would not necessarily be formidable, for in a city like Philadelphia, New York, or Chicago, he would find perhaps all the variety requisite for the awakening of his inventive powers, and the knocking out of his conceit, if this were a part of his kit. Now why don't we produce more geniuses from the classes with *better* educations?

De Tocqueville wrote in 1840 concerning America in this connection:

" It must be admitted that, among the civilized peoples of our time, there are few in which the higher sciences have made less progress than in the United States."

And continuing he adds:

" I consider the people of the United States as that portion of the English people which is charged with the exploitation of the forests of the new world, while the rest of the nation, enjoying more leisure and less preoccupied with the material needs of life, may devote itself to thought and to the development of the human mind in every field."

It is true that this statement of De Tocqueville was written many years ago, but he points out a truth still more or less applicable to conditions today in the pursuit of wealth, with its strenuous preoccupation.

Tyndall wrote in this connection as follows:

" If great scientific results are not achieved in America, it is not to the small agitations of society that I should be disposed to ascribe the defect; but to the fact that the men among you who possess the endowments necessary for profound scientific enquiry, are laden with duties of administration, so heavy as to be utterly incompatible with the conditions and tranquil meditation which original investigation demands."

This criticism of Tyndall still holds in full force today, and is undoubtedly one of the prime

CHARLES EDWARD MUNROE

Chemist, Inventor of Smokeless Powder

Born at Cambridge, Mass., May 24th, 1849. S.B. Harvard, 1871, Ph.D. Columbian (now George Washington University), 1894, Assistant in Chemistry, Harvard, 1871 to 1874; Professor of Chemistry United States Naval Academy, 1874 to 1886; Chemist to Torpedo Corps, United States Naval Torpedo Station and War College, 1886 to 1892; Head Professor of Chemistry, 1892 — Dean Corcoran Scientific School, 1892 to 1898, Dean Faculty of Graduate Studies, 1893 —, George Washington University.

Consulting Expert of Engineer's Board on Defense of Washington, 1898; Expert Special Agent in Charge Chemical Industries of the U. S. for Censuses of 1900, 1905, and 1910; Consulting expert United States Geological Survey, United States Bureau of Mines, and Civil Service Commission; Chairman Advisory Committee American Railroad Association for Drafting of Regulations Governing Transportation of Explosives, 1905.

Appointed by Swedish Academy of Sciences, 1900, to nominate candidate for Nobel Prizes in Chemistry.

Inventor of Smokeless Powder and authority on explosives; Chairman Committee on Explosives Investigations, Council of National Defense; author of over 100 books and papers on chemistry and explosives.

Commandant Order of Medjidieh, Turkey, 1901. Fellow Chemical Society, London, American Academy of Arts and Sciences, Society of Chemical Industry England; President American Chemical Society, 1898 to 1899; Chairman Committee on Explosives American Society for Testing Materials.

reasons why America doesn't know its greatest men, at least its greatest scientific men.

A rough and ready life in a country to be conquered, however, has great developing value if the worker is not *overworked*. Reference has frequently been made as to how and why the youth on a farm usually excel in later years, and I think that as far as invention goes, the stimulus is due to the fact that a self-contained farm is in a sense a complete manufacturing plant, a laboratory and a forum of combined activity of mind and body. In earlier days every farmstead was a very complete and self-contained manufacturing plant, from the fabrication of candles to the spinning of the wool raised at hand, the making of the rough homespun cloth, and the driving of the well, and the crystal water from its depths, the meat consumed, the poultry and the eggs, the butter, milk and cream were all products of the self-contained establishment. Fruits in season were preserved, all vegetables necessary were homegrown, ice was cut from the pond on the premises and stored for the summer's need, and the fuel wood was sawed and hauled to the woodshed for the winter's use. The ashes left from the great wood fires were kept with the waste fat from the table for the making of soft soap by the combination of the potash steeped from the ashes with water and the greasy table savings referred to. A complete listing of science on the farm would, of course, be interesting in itself, but I prefer here rather to devote the space at hand to the human side of inventive work, and to impress the principle, that if a man is too heavily burdened with routine work, the world loses many of its ablest men. Charles Josiah Golpin depicts most beautifully an overworked farmer, possibly the father of little James Watt, who devised the great steam engine from the teakettle on the stove. " The arena of country life, labor, and struggle, where the farmer and his family achieve the primary habits of thought and action, is the farmstead." The farmer, continues Golpin, " is the man, hoe in hand, with bent back, striking blow after blow at the weakest point in the earth's crust, pulling upward, loosening the earth's grip upon a portion of the soil, lifting it for a moment, and finally turning it upon its face. This momentary mechanical victory is repeated, clod by clod, yard by yard, hour after hour, day after day, all through the season of soil preparation. Unremittingly looking his earth antagonist in the eye, the land-worker gives and takes — gives his blows and takes the after-effects into his own body and soul." How can such a man, however he may be intellectually endowed, rise above the routine and bodily fatigue? Yet we

see the same principle in the hard routine work
of the scholar, forced into finance and account-
ing, duties of management and administration.
And if he is rich in worldly things, is he the
owner, or do these worldly things own him,
body and soul? Can a man today own a million, or does the million own the man, and here
I am speaking of the man with the inventive
and research type of mind. For the man with
the passion for owning more and more, the
money fiend, the world doesn't care which is
the owner in this type, the man or his money,
but the world is after all the loser, for many
of the money grabbers are simply men made
of good stuff led astray. They lose their balance, and their sense of proportion as to the
value of gold. There will always be the passion for acquiring; it is, according to the psychologists, as we have seen, a natural impulse.
" It is impossible," says Morgan, in his work
upon Ancient Society, " to overestimate the influence of property in the civilization of mankind. It was the power that brought the Aryan
and Semitic nations out of barbarism into civilization. The growth of the idea of property in
the human mind commenced in feebleness and
ended in becoming its master passion. Governments and laws are instituted with primary
reference to its creation, protection, and en-
joyment. It introduced human slavery in its

production; and after the experience of several thousand years, it caused the abolition of slavery upon the discovery that the free man was a better property-making machine." Mark this last sentence, that the free man was a better property-making machine. Does this not indicate that if more of our men were freer from the slavery of routine over burdensome duties, that they would become better property-making machines? The ideal to the writer's mind is to clearly predetermine how much may be necessary for happiness, secure this amount, and then devote one's time to those vocations which bring out one's best. I know of no happier illustration than the balanced working conditions and ambitions to acquire property as the result of his labors than that of the great French chemist, Antoine Laurent Lavoisier. He was born in Paris in 1743, and when he was only twenty-one years old, he devised novel ways and means for the lighting of city streets, and was awarded the national prize by the French Government. The Academy of Sciences elected him a member when he was twenty-five. Lavoisier was the first to show that sulphur, in burning, increases in weight; that is to say, from one pound of sulphur much more than one pound of vitriolic acid is produced, without taking into account the natural moisture in the air. The thoroughness and accuracy of Lavoisier's work brought French chemistry great fame. By one of his experiments he proved that the alchemical notion of the transmutation of water into earth was erroneous. Lavoisier published in 1784 a volume entitled "Essays Physical and Chemical," setting forth all that had been accomplished on the subject of airs from the time of Paracelsus to 1774, and included also an account of his own brilliant work wherein he established the fundamental fact that a metal burns with the absorption of air, and that when the metallic calc is strongly heated in the presence of charcoal, an air is set free which is of the same nature as the fixed air of Dr. Black.

Lavoisier deposited with the Secretary of the Academy of Science in 1772 a sealed note, and this note was not opened until the 1st day of May, 1773.

Here are the contents of this historic communication to the famous Academy:

" About eight days ago I discovered that sulphur in burning, far from losing, augments in weight; that is to say, that from one pound of sulphur much more than one pound of vitriolic acid is obtained, without reckoning the humidity of the air. Phosphorus presents the same phenomenon. This augmentation of weight arises from a great quantity of air which becomes fixed during the combustion, and which combines with the vapors.

" This discovery, confirmed by experiments which I regard as decisive, led me to think that what is observed in the combustion of sulphur and phosphorus might likewise take place with respect to all bodies which augment in weight by combustion and calcination; and I was persuaded that the augmentation of weight in the calcs of metals proceeded from the same cause. The experiments fully confirmed my conjectures.

"I operated the reduction of litharge in closed vessels with Hale's apparatus, and I observed that at the moment of the passage of the calcs into the metallic state, there was a disengagement of air in considerable quantity, and that this air formed a volume at least one thousand times greater than that of the litharge employed.

" As this discovery appears to me one of the most interesting which has been made since Stahl, I thought it expedient to secure to myself the property by depositing the present note in the hands of the Secretary of the Academy, to remain secret till the period when I shall publish my experiments."

LAVOISIER

Paris, 11 November, 1772

This great French chemist was an industrious worker, a contributor to the world's knowledge; and his interest in fortune was very secondary to his passion of research.

great opportunity to make amends with full and telling force.

" The time has come," writes Dr. J. S. Ames, "for America to recognize the usefulness of the scholar, the thinker, the investigator of science. All the other countries of the world have done so long since." And in an address of recent date delivered before the students of the University of Virginia upon the subject of our part in the great war, he said: — " I think it only fair to say that the universities of this country have played their part well.

"Before we actually entered this war, in those anxious years when we were waiting to see whether we would be given an opportunity to join in the fight for the cause of honor, freedom and the teachings of Christianity, or whether we must walk through the years of our lives with heads hung in disgrace, no group of people did as much to hold aloft the illuminating torch, revealing the iniquity of the enemy of civilization, as did the presidents of our universities. Theirs will be the honor forever. They who would not keep silent. Then, as soon as we were by official act in a state of war, the first to step forward and say 'Use me' were the faculties and student bodies."

Let us trace the development of the scholarly thinker in science and follow the spirit of research here down to our own great awakening possibilities.

Research in America, it must be appreciated, is naturally a very recent art, but research in the old world dates back to the dark ages, and its inception is lost in the mists of antiquity.

In the middle ages, however, the records are clear, for the Hermit Philosophers, better known perhaps as the Alchemists, dwelt and cast their spirit of research about them in almost every town and city of Europe, and down through the centuries which followed, the life principle of science and philosophy impregnated the teachings of all college faculties.

And in connection with early research, even before the discovery of America, we should not overplay the customary belittling of Alchemy. Its advocates were at times sincere and painstaking. As interpreted in the words of a great chemical philosopher, "Alchemy was never at any time anything different from chemistry."

And so we see that France, England and Italy, Scandinavia and Germany, and the other countries of the old world had the early fostering influence for research of the Alchemists, and of the earliest subsequent students in the more stable sciences.

Since the writer's early education was received in schools in France, England and Germany, the spirit of painstaking research in the Universities and even in the high schools abroad was evident to him and naturally made its first and lasting impression.

In Germany, under compulsory education laws, within the black-white-red painted boundary posts, so familiar to those who have visited and studied the Empire, I remember that the spirit of text-books and inquiry into the facts and forces of nature were so strongly fostered, that the boys in the streets of German cities would often know the names of great scientists and other renowned scholars, and not the names of the strong men who toyed with massive weights in the public squares, or the national gamesters. I mention this to bring out the fact that Germany has never been a nation of sportsmen, but rather one of abnormally close and painstaking application, and when I was a student in Munich, I could not fail to observe and record how morbidly close the German stuck to his studies.

No engineer who has been to Germany and studied and traveled there can fail to appreciate that her great strength during the war lay in the foundation of her organized research, and that in the absence of a true and fair sporting spirit, she was without conscience as to ways and means or method. But she was devilishly thorough in the theory and practice of her research. Here is but one incident which will illustrate the point. In a recent con-

versation with the president of an American
steel company with whom I had to do in the
manufacture of war munitions, he informed me
that his supply of vanadium for the making of
vanadium alloy steels had been cut off from the
supply in South America through the poisoning
of the llamas employed in bringing the vanadium ore down through the hazardous passes
in their mountainous country.

And may it not be asked, — unless German
education has been decidedly faulty, how can
one account for the unmanly and unmilitary
use of poison gas and the countless other horrors developed and introduced into the war by
German scientists? Was it necessary that university and profound research education and
efficient organization should have been accompanied by a general debasement of moral
character?

I think not, for there were no more brilliant
workers in science, for example, than the
French, and there was scarcely a great city or
a little town in the other countries of Europe
before the war, without its university and its
studious staff of professors and assistants at
work upon the great problems of nature.

It has been a mistaken notion that the
French and the British did not produce research
technologists just as keen and just as able as
Germany, even in the most complex organic

chemistry of dyeing, which has often been regarded as a German art. When the great art of
dyeing was young, the academic and practical
honors were by no means all Germany's.

In the famous International Exposition in
London, in 1862, the chemical genius in producing intricate coal-tar products was mainly
French and English. Here the United King-
dom received 12 medals by the International
Jury of Award, and France received 21, and
Germany and Austria together only 12. The
genius and skill were all there with France and
England, but for some reason or another they
did not sustain the competitive *commercial*
spirit.

And in America, it must be remembered
that at the beginning of the present century
there were practically no laboratories equipped
for general instruction in chemistry and physics comparable with those abroad.

There were, to be sure, science courses to
be had at certain of our colleges, but principally
lecture courses, and chemistry and physics
were often conjoined with mineralogy and
anatomy, and unlike the great universities
abroad, very few students here ever were
privileged to receive first-hand knowledge, by
men who had done great things themselves.
The greatest teachers for inspiring students
should have known how to advance alone into

regions where no other man has ever broken ground. "He must have worked upon the frontiers of human knowledge and conquered for himself new domains."

It has been too often the case that classrooms were filled with students here who only listened to lectures, and often to lectures delivered by lecturers who had never had any practical experience with the subjects with which they were dealing.

And the same objection pertained often to the writers of American books, for alas only too often an author would write a book, and a text book too, with only second-hand knowledge.

It was not uncommon to hear fallacies repeated by different lecturers, and to find the same errors relating to scientific phenomena copied from one text book into another, none of the authors having first-hand knowledge about the subject, or he would not have stupidly described an experiment, or set forth a process.

Then again a college professor in America has for years been the subject of jokes and been likened to dancing masters, tonsorial artists, and confused with men who, dressed in tights and spangles, come down successfully in parachutes after balloon ascensions at county fairs. I think it was George Ade who described a professor over here as one who goes up in a balloon, and when he comes down, if his friend who is waiting for him won't lend him ten dollars, threatens to tell the wife about a bracelet he once bought in Akron, Ohio.

"A professor with us," writes Dr. W. R. Whitney, "is a conscientious alumnus a little older than his assistants. He is stunting his mental growth on a salary that no chauffeur would accept. He is not expected to be a scientist, nor a worker in science. He is not asked to show boys how new things may be done by doing them. He must confine himself to talking about accomplishments of others, usually foreigners. We rail at him, but do not help him at all. The fault is not his. He was raised as a part of the system which we, in our poverty, had but to employ."

When I returned to America from one of my early trips abroad I was asked to coöperate with certain others interested in research at home, by canvassing congressmen and in explaining the crying need, and to urge the passage of the bill just introduced at the time providing for our National Bureau of Standards.

I had often visited the extensive Laboratoire D'Essais in Paris, the French National Research organization, and the great Physikalisch-Technische Reichsanstalt, the Imperial German Bureau of Standards and Research at

Charlottenburg, near Berlin, and when I came home I was deeply mortified in my knowledge that we had absolutely nothing whatever to compare with these institutions in America, nor anything at all comparable with the extensive National Physical Laboratories at Teddington, near London.

To be specific, all we had in America was three men at work in four rooms, in connection with the Coast and Geodetic Survey at Washington, engaged in standardizing weights and measures, and that at Yale University they were calibrating, for a fee, the little clinical thermometers into true degrees, for the use of physicians and surgeons.

I am told that the Weather Bureau, once in a while, made some kind of a test for a fee for some commercial concern when the test was of such simple nature that it could be undertaken.

"You are advocating just another Bureau with more salaries," I was promptly told by a lawyer-politician, with no appreciation of the importance of the subject in hand. I made the rounds of both houses of Congress and collected some very remarkable comments, mostly in strong and short-sighted opposition.

These gentlemen knew nothing of the great Laboratoire D'Essais, or of the National Laboratories at London, or of the Reichsanstalt, and cared less, but there were a few, however, who became educated to the need and the possibilities of such an establishment, and after much hard work by many champions of the cause, the bill was passed, in 1901, with broad functions, wholly consistent with modern views of standards, standard measurements and research.

We have today a majestic plant and a very efficient organization under the Directorship of Dr. S. W. Stratton and this comparatively recent bureau, which has grown additionally during the war, ranks in importance with our other and older Federal institutions.

If we are now to acquire research efficiency, we cannot lapse into stupid indifference, and continue to elect corruptible or anti-American politicians and place them at the helm in affairs of state, industry and commerce. I am inclined to think that we are awake now, and that we will not be caught napping again. Dissemination of German gold as a powerful part of German propaganda before the war to admit German dyes and dyestuffs is now only one of the many well-established facts which have been uncovered, and if our eyes are really opened we must prepare at once to fight educationally and scientifically, instituting an intensive and aggressive campaign. We have learned to our mortification that no defensive bulwark, in the form of a tariff, no matter how high, will answer as protection. We must equip for the battle and stand upon our feet and fight to capture and to hold. Reliance upon protection, or hoping to thrive on the boycotting of German goods, now that the war is won, would be an inexcusable lapsing into old lamented methods. I can here testify first hand, from contact with many American manufacturers, that a great majority of them belittled academically trained technologists, and when they employed them at all, they were regarded as a highly expensive and speculative investment. While Germany was building some of her greatest and most substantial industries, destined to shine as unchallenged examples to the entire world, Great Britain and America did not appreciate the soundness of their slumbers. In old England, I have been told that chemists were not favored, because, "knowing something about the business, they might influence it in some way."

Sir Joseph Lamar pointed out that England had no use for chemists, but that Germany regarded them as the highest of assets, and that the present war is one of chemists, and that the coming peace will likewise be one of chemists. Professor Armstrong wrote in the London "Times" his views and experiences in England also. "Though I have fifty years' experience as a chemist," he writes, "particularly in connection with the materials being used in the manufacture of explosives and of natural and artificial organic products, I have never been consulted; and the only request for my assistance that I have received, since the outbreak of the war, came from a German gentleman, long since naturalized as a British subject. No doubt I am properly regarded as merely a retired professor, but I know highly competent younger men among those trained by me who are equally unutilized."

The industrial plan in Germany was ever fundamentally based upon research and organization — an organization designed to expand against all the counter forces of more inert nations, until she achieved her policy of world domination. And in this grand scheme of organization for military victory as well as industrial control, it may now be seen how the university played a most important part, and how the professors, the Herr Professors, the Herr Doctor Professors and the Herr Doctor Lecturer Professors, and the Herr Doctor Lecturer Research Professors, threw their might into the great balance of her progressive scheme.

While German factories were regarding such men as their principal assets, and were not afraid to coöperate by an orderly exchange of technical information, we and our English cousins ran our factories in a comparatively slipshod manner, without adequate scientific management or control, and instead of the co-operative spirit one saw in Germany, there existed on the contrary the fiercest competitive spirit.

We have been indifferent, or else we have emphasized the selfish inefficient individualism, while Germany has taught organized and efficient scientific coöperation.

One used to hear in America when we had a chemical problem which might be solved by doing a little rational and intensive work upon it: — " Let's hire a Dutch chemist and set him to work," and often we would do so, and in ignorance of, or indifference to, the elaborate system of highly organized commercial espionage by using strategic positions, at salaries that "no chauffeur would accept," because these chemists we employed from the other side of the water drew pay *sub rosa*, from the secret service of the Imperial German Government.

Any engineer who has traveled abroad in connection with technology, and who has recorded the difference in methods as practiced here, cannot fail to appreciate what we have suffered through American indifference. And this indifference was not confined to the tech-

nology of peace, for in the great arts and
sciences of national defense we were especially
sleepy and indifferent.

Not having chosen a strain of praise for our
national activities in the previous pages of this
little book, I am here giving one or two personal
experiences, which I trust will show that I
am not unpatriotic, but on the contrary that I
have done my best at all times toward awakening American research efficiency through pa-
triotic motive and during the past few years
more particularly in National Defense. It was
early in May, 1914, about three months before
the breaking out of the world war, that I tried
in vain to secure interest and backing for introducing elaborate illustrated educational lecture courses dealing with the need for a greater
and more scientific defense for America on
land and sea.

I approached many wealthy and enlightened
Americans in quest of support of such a movement, but I failed utterly to find anyone who
would put up a dollar outside of the steel,
munition, and ship-building interests, and these
interests I did not enlist for fear of misunder-
standings and criticisms.

Having failed to secure "disinterested"
capital and having steered clear of "interested" capital, I started the introduction of
semi-technical illustrated lectures dealing with

the science and engineering of national defense on my own hook, and financed the undertaking independently.

I wished to throw my little mite into the balance, advocating preparedness, and I started out with the Building of the Navy along the lines recommended by the Navy League of the United States, and I prepared and gave the lectures with the endorsement of this organization.

Having been Electrical Engineer for the Navy Department for several years, I was in close touch with this arm of the national defense and all its works, as well as with the naval administration. I had given practical talks at the Seaman Gunner's School at the Washington Navy Yard, and had been to sea on battleships and destroyers with the sanction of the Secretary of the Navy to make notes, photographs and motion pictures, and I covered as far as possible every phase of inspiring interest from constructive material of a scientific nature to the training of the men and their life at sea.

We had also secured dissolving views and motion pictures of iron and steel making, in rolling armor plate, in the building of great guns, in the making and testing of smokeless powder and high explosives, mines, torpedoes, and ships, and we hired theaters, placarded towns, put up electric signs, distributed circulars, and advertised in all the daily newspapers where we were presenting the lectures.

Prominent people with wealth and influence were invited to attend, and were presented with boxes and orchestra chairs, and prominent speakers were announced as drawing cards, but it was not possible to awaken interest.

Very few indeed responded. " We licked the British in '76 " was the complacent voice of the nation.

In one of our largest cities, I hired the biggest and most impressive theater, put up electric signs, placarded the town with colored posters, distributed literature, and advertised and secured write-ups in all the newspapers of the city. The lecture was upon the United States Navy and the great Sciences and Arts in its Development.

On the night of the lecture there was a little heaven-born band of about fifteen people clustered in the orchestra chairs in the center of the house and two or three in the galleries, and I recognized quite a number in the audience as being personal friends who had come either through curiosity or through staunch friendship's sake, or through a composite mixture of both, and I struggled with the lantern operator and the address to the best of my ability.

At the close of the lecture the manager of

the theater came to me and said, "This has been a frightful frost, sir, and I can't tell you how mortified I feel."

"You don't feel half as mortified as I do," I replied, and then a sinking feeling came over me when I realized that I had hired and contracted for the theater for the following night also, and had elaborately advertised a second lecture. What on earth could be done to save the day? My personal manager, who by the way was my brother, was possessed with as much humor as administrative capacity, and he became inspired with a bright idea, and the following morning bright and early his bright idea was put into practice.

He collected all of the tickets which were lying fallow in the box office, and taking them out in a hand-bag, he distributed them through the courtesy of the floor-walkers in the five and ten cent stores for the use of the salesmen and sales ladies, and among all the other cheaper department stores of the city, and then he went to the police department, the fire department and the street cleaning department, and he announced that it would be a great motion picture show, the first ever given in the most fashionable theater of the city.

It was during that period in our national history when motion pictures were confined within the ill-ventilated four walls of a transformed

shoe store with a false front, and it was the
first time in the annals of the city that the
great Lyceum Theater was advertised for a
motion picture show, and furthermore the report was circulated that we were going to advertise by giving away canary birds and silk
stockings.

When I stepped out upon the broad stage of
the Lyceum Theater the following night, with
its boxes and balconies all decorated with
flags and palms, I looked into a great sea of
expectant faces.

In the boxes were stout ladies with waving
plumes in their hair, and gentlemen in pre-
historic dress suits, elaborate studies in fans,
frills and feathers, variegated colored gowns,
pink satin ties and diamond shirt studs.

In the packed orchestra chairs there were
men and women old and middle aged in holi-
day attire, fellows with their very bestest
girls, lovers quietly content, grannys, cousins,
uncles, sisters and aunts, and each and every
one of them wearing that delightful expression
worn by our countrymen about to receive
something for nothing.

We had through hard labor, and the science
of psychology, " put one over " on our countrymen, and at last I had secured an audience!

I exploited the navy in words and pictures
from its early history down through the era of
the towering wooden ships of the line of battle

which through the skill and courage of their commanders and crews, the art of sailing and grim cast iron guns, ruled the seas, to our own age of modern wonders. We dealt with the spirit of Drake and Nelson and John Paul Jones, and I showed them pictures and gave them descriptions all the way from the making of a sailor to the manufacture of armor-plate and high explosives. We had motion pictures covering every phase of naval life and naval science from the training of the men to the making and testing of model ships in model testing basins, and motion pictures of target practice with great guns, and the work and possibilities of the torpedo and submarine.

A free and open forum of discussion was invited, and after the lecture, which was courteously and attentively listened to, many came up upon the stage.

A big fellow, a captain of police from the fifth precinct, to whom we had sent a box, said in a proprietary manner, " I wouldn't have come if I had understood it was to be a lecture, but I will say that we all enjoyed your *pictures*, and he emphasized the word "pictures" with considerable meaning, " but," he asked just as he was leaving, " I would like to know what you get out of all this! "

"I get a great deal out of it," I replied, " or I wouldn't do it."

"Yes, yes, yes, I know," he said, "but from just whom, — the moneyed interests backing this propaganda, the steel plants, the armor-plate makers, the powder factories, or the politicians advocating the spending of the people's money?"

When I assured him that I had received no compensation whatever, except the great pleasure of talking to such an interested and intelligent audience, he left scratching his head in very dubious thoughts.

Six weeks later I left for England, Germany and Russia, and became engulfed in the great war. After intimately witnessing several months of the conflict with Germany, I returned to the United States, and was so infuriated with what I saw of German brutality in Belgium, that I lectured again on National Defense, at times finding it impossible without breaking the decree of neutrality, until the United States joined the Allies.

During the first week of our country's participation, I offered my services to the President, and ever since, up to the closing of the war, I have enjoyed the greatest variety of absorbing scientific war problems, and have been privileged to associate with many of the greatest scientific minds who were not only from the various institutions of learning in our country, but with those brilliant technologists

CHAPTER IV

American War Research

ONE of the most inspiring and picturesque figures in early American war science was that of our great Joseph Henry at work in the art of military signaling during those anxious and uncertain days of the war between the States.

Often accompanied in the blackness of the night by his friend and ardent admirer, Abraham Lincoln, he climbed the lofty brownstone watch tower of the Smithsonian Institution, where he directed certain experiments in flashlight signaling.

Chief among American foundations of science and research at this time, was the new National Academy of Sciences of which Henry was one of the leading spirits. Founded during the strife of the Civil War and approved by President Lincoln, the National Academy served during this unhappy period in our history as the scientific adviser to the United States Government, and reported to the Departments of War and Navy its views and recommendations on the scientific problems involved in the military and naval arts.

The bill incorporating the National Academy of Sciences was introduced on February 21, 1863. The bill passed through Congress without delay and was executed by President Lincoln on March 3.

Not only because of the historic interest to American Science and Research, but because of what developed from this organization in America's part in the great world war, the draft of the original bill setting forth its founders is given here.

An Act to Incorporate the National Academy of Sciences

Be it enacted by the Senate and House of Representatives of the United States of America in Congress assembled, that Louis Agassiz, Massachusetts; J. H. Alexander, Maryland; S. Alexander, New Jersey; A. D. Bache, at large; F. A. P. Barnard, at large; J. G. Barnard, United States Army, Massachusetts; W. H. C. Bartlett, United States Military Academy, Missouri; U. A. William Boyden, Massachusetts; Alexis Caswell, Rhode Island; William Chauvenet, Missouri; J. H. C. Coffin, United States Naval Academy, Maine; J. A. Dahlgren, United States Navy, Pennsylvania; J. D.

Dana, Connecticut; Charles H. Davis, United States Navy, Massachusetts; George Engelmann, St. Louis, Missouri; J. F. Frazer, Pennsylvania; Wolcott Gibbs, New York; J. M. Gilliss, United States Navy, Kentucky; A. A. Gould, Massachusetts; B. A. Gould, Massachusetts; Asa Gray, Massachusetts; A. Guyot, New Jersey; James Hall, New York; Joseph Henry, at large; J. E. Hilgard, at large; Illinois; Edward Hitchcock, Massachusetts; J. S. Hubbard, United States Naval Observatory, Connecticut; A. A. Humphreys, United States Army, Pennsylvania; J. L. LeConte, United States Army, Pennsylvania; J. Leidy, Pennsylvania; P. J. Lesley, Pennsylvania; M. S. Longstreth, Pennsylvania; D. H. Mahan, United States Military Academy, Virginia; J. S. Newberry, Ohio; H. A. Newton, Connecticut; Benjamin Peirce, Massachusetts; John Rogers, United States Navy, Indiana; Fairman Rogers, Pennsylvania; R. E. Rogers, Pennsylvania; W. B. Rogers, Massachusetts; L. M. Rutherford, New York; Joseph Saxton, at large; Benjamin Silliman, Connecticut; Benjamin Silliman, Junior, Connecticut; Theodore Strong, New Jersey; John Torrey, New York; J. G. Totten, United States Army, Connecticut; Joseph Winlock, United States Nautical Almanac, Kentucky; Jeffries Wyman, Massachusetts; J. W. Whitney, California, their associates and successors, duly chosen, are hereby incorporated, constituted and declared to be a body corporate, by the name of the National Academy of Sciences.

Section 2. And be it further enacted, that the National Academy of Sciences shall consist of not more than fifty ordinary members, and the said corporation hereby constituted shall have power to make its own organization, including its constitution, by-laws, and rules and regulations; to fill all vacancies created by death, resignation, or otherwise; to provide for the election of foreign and domestic members, the division into classes, and all other matters needful or usual in such institutions, and to report the same to Congress.

Section 3. And be it further enacted, that the National Academy of Sciences shall hold an annual meeting at such place in the United States as may be designated, and the Academy shall, whenever called upon by any department of the Government, investigate, examine, experiment and report upon any subject of science or art, the actual expense of such investigations, examinations, experiments, and reports to be paid for from appropriations which may be made for the purpose; but the academy shall receive no compensation whatever for any services to the Government of the United States.

Solomon Foote

President of the Senate pro tempore

Galusha A. Grow

Speaker of the House of Representatives

Approved, March 23, 1863

Abraham Lincoln, *President*

This interesting pioneer bill has subsequently been amended to remove the limitation of membership, and to permit the Academy to receive bequests. The Academy now elects fifteen new members annually and has adopted a less conservative and a more progressive spirit.

The following partial list of papers printed, and problems reported upon, is given here as a matter of historic as well as technical interest and to indicate by contrast their comparative simplicity with the polytechnics of the great world war just closed.

Joseph Henry: On Materials for Combustion of Lamps in Lighthouses.

W. H. C. Bartlett: On Rifle Guns.

F. A. P. Barnard: On the Force of Fired Gunpowder and the Pressure to which Heavy Guns are actually Subjected in Firing.

ELIHU THOMSON
Electrician, Inventor of Electric Welding

Born Manchester, England, March 29th, 1853. Degree of A.B. Central High School, Philadelphia, 1870, A.M. 1875; (Honorary A.M. Yale, 1890; Ph.D. Tufts, 1894; Sc.D. Harvard, 1909); Professor of Chemistry and Mechanics Central High School, Philadelphia, 1870 to 1880; since 1880 Electrician for Thomson-Houston, and General Electric Companies, which operate under his inventions, more than 500 patents; inventor of Electric Welding, which bears his name, and many other important inventions in electric lighting power, etc. Member of many American and foreign electrical engineering and scientific societies; Honorary Member of Institution of Electrical Engineers of Great Britain; President of International Electrical Congress and of chamber of Official Delegates thereto, St. Louis, 1904; President International Electrochemical Commission, 1908 to 1911; Fellow American Academy of Arts and Sciences, Vice President; Member of National Academy of Sciences.

Awarded Grand Prix in Paris, 1889, and 1900 for Electrical Inventions; Decorated 1889 by French Government, Chevalier and Officier Legion of Honor, for Electrical Research and Invention: Grand Prize St. Louis, 1904 for Electrical Work; Rumford Medal, 1902; awarded first Edison Medal, American Institute of Electrical Engineers, 1910; Elliott Cresson Medal, John Fritz Medal, and Hughes Medal of Royal Society London, 1916, etc.

Trustee Peabody Academy of Science, Salem, Mass.; Member Corporation Massachusetts Institute of Technology, Boston. Member National Research Council.

B. A. Gould: A Number of Papers pertaining to the Stature, Proportions, Ages, and Vision of American Soldiers.

J. E. Hilgard: On a Chronograph for measuring the Velocity of Projectiles.

Among the reports made to the United States Government by the National Academy of Sciences are the following:

On the Protection of Bottoms of Iron Vessels from Corrosion.

On the Adjustment of Compasses to Correct Magnetic Deviation in Iron Ships.

On Wind and Current Charts and Sailing Directions.

On the Explosion on the United States Steamer *Chenango.*

On Experiments on the Expansion of Steam.

On the Preservation of Paint on Army Knapsacks.

But the stupendous problems of the present great war and the endless task in solving them naturally dwarf these early plans and labors of men into comparative insignificance, leading us moreover into the most complex and often cumbersome organizations. After witnessing two years of terrific combat between the Central and Allied Powers on land and sea, using engines of devastation undreamed of in the annals of science, and with no clear vision into the horrors of possible outcome,

President Wilson was led to believe during
this world wide conflagration of peace and
safety, that American technology should, as
developed abroad, be in some manner expanded into greater fields and mobilized.

The National Research Council

From the valuable service rendered by such
men as Joseph Henry and his fellow charter
members and associates in the National Academy of Sciences during the Civil War, and
from the provisions of its charter for assisting
the Government in investigating, examining,
experimenting and reporting upon any subject
of science or art, it was pointed out that it
constituted logically the nucleus for greater
activities in the world war.

During the month of April, 1916, President
Wilson was led to express the wish that the
National Academy of Sciences should act as
such a nucleus and coördinate the educational and industrial and other research agencies with the Government. Dr. George Ellery
Hale, in an able address under the auspices of
the Engineering Foundation in the Engineering Societies' Building, in New York in May,
1918, set forth the steps in the formation of the
National Research Council, of which he was
Chairman, as follows: — "The Academy's con-

nection with the Government, its inclusion of the whole range of science, and its many years of coöperation with the Royal Society of London, the Paris Academy of Sciences, and other similar academies abroad, pointed to it as the only body in the United States in a position to comply with the President's request.

It was clear, however, that membership in the desired organization should not be exclusively confined to the National Academy. Many technical bureaus of the Army and Navy, for example, should be represented by their chiefs *ex-officiis*, and in other cases a changing membership, broadly representative of research in its numerous aspects, would also be desirable. The Organizing Committee accordingly recommended the establishment of a new body, resting legally upon the character of the Academy, sharing its privileges, both at home and abroad, and at the same time affording the wide freedom of selection desired.

The National Research Council, comprising the chiefs of the technical bureaus of the Army and Navy, the heads of Government bureaus engaged in scientific research, a group of investigators representing educational institutions and research foundations, and another group including representatives of industrial and engineering research, was accordingly constituted by the Academy with the active co-operation of the leading national scientific and engineering societies.

On July 24, 1916, President Wilson addressed a letter to the President of the National Academy expressing his approval of a preliminary report regarding the National Research Council, and promising his coöperation and that of the various departments of the Government.

Since that time he has continued to give his support to the work of the Research Council, and has appointed various representatives of the Government to membership in it.

On February 28, 1917, the Council of National Defense passed a resolution expressing its recognition of the fact that the National Research Council, at the request of the President, had organized the scientific resources of the country in the interest of national defense and national welfare, and requesting the Research Council to coöperate with it in matters pertaining to scientific research for national defense.

As a result of this action the Chairman of the Council opened offices in the Munsey Building in March, and entered into active coöperation with the Council of National Defense, which was then established in the same building.

Soon afterwards the Research Council was

requested to act as the Department of Science and Research of the Council of National Defense, in which capacity it has continued to serve for the organization of investigations on military and industrial problems and, in harmony with the expressed wish of the President, as an agency for securing widespread co-operation in the field of science and research.

A further extension of the duties of the National Research Council occurred in July, when it was requested by the Chief Signal Officer to organize a Division of Science and Research of the Signal Corps. Major (now Lieutenant Colonel) Robert A. Milliken was placed in charge of this Division, which has remained in close contact with the Research Council, engaged in the solution of numerous problems of military importance.

Another important request on behalf of the Government, made by Assistant Secretary of War Stettinius, resulted in the appointment of a Committee of the Research Council to organize and direct extensive researches for the improvement of processes for the fixation of nitrogen, undertaken in coöperation with the Ordnance Department of the Army."

Then the National Research Council reached far out and embraced the universities and other educational institutions equipped for original research, and to show the widespread plans and the method of reaching laboratories and men, I am giving here the letter received from the president of the university in Washington with which I have the honor to be affiliated.

THE GEORGE WASHINGTON UNIVERSITY
WASHINGTON, D.C.

Office of
    The President   February 8, 1917

Professor N. Monroe Hopkins,
        2128 Bancroft Place,
                Washington, D.C.

Sir:

The following is the first paragraph of a letter received by me from Dr. George E. Hale, Chairman of the National Research Council:

"The purpose of the National Research Council, which has been formed at the request of the President of the United States by the National Academy of Sciences, is to bring into coöperation governmental, educational, industrial, and other research organizations with the object of encouraging the investigation of natural phenomena, the increased use of scientific research in the development of American industries, the employment of scientific methods in strengthening the national defense, and such other applications of science as will promote the national security and welfare.

"In pursuance of these aims, the Committee on Research in Educational Institutions has recommended the establishment of a Research Committee in each educational institution according serious support to original investigations in science on the part of members of the faculty and advanced students."

In response to this request I have appointed you a member of the Committee on Research for the George Washington University. A list of the Committee will be found enclosed.

Yours very truly,

C. H. Stockton

President

Thus it may be seen how the National Research Council grew in response to the needs of the nation, and because of its permanent place and position in American research, I am including in the present chapter the text of the Executive order pertaining thereto.

Executive Order of President Wilson

The National Research Council was organized in 1916 at the request of the President by the National Academy of Sciences, under its congressional charter, as a measure of national preparedness. The work accomplished by the Council in organizing research and in securing coöperation of military and civilian agencies in the solution of military problems demonstrated its capacity for large service. The National Academy of Sciences is therefore requested to perpetuate the National Research Council, the duties of which shall be as follows:

1. In general, to stimulate research in the mathematical, physical and biological sciences, and in the application of these sciences to engineering, agriculture, medicine and other useful arts, with the object of increasing knowledge, of strengthening the national defense, and in contributing in other ways to the public welfare.

2. To survey the larger possibilities of science, to formulate comprehensive projects of research, and to develop effective means of utilizing the scientific and technical resources of the country for dealing with these projects.

3. To promote coöperation in research, at home and abroad, in order to secure concentration of effort, minimize duplication and stimulate progress; but in all coöperative undertakings to give encouragement to individual initiative, as fundamentally important to the advancement of science.

4. To serve as a means of bringing American and foreign investigators into active coöperation with the scientific and technical services of the War and Navy Departments and with those of civil branches of the Government.

5. To direct the attention of scientific and technical investigators to the present impor-

tance of military and industrial problems in connection with the war, and to aid in the solution of these problems by organizing specific researches.

6. To gather and collate scientific and technical information at home and abroad, in coöperation with Governmental and other agencies and to render such information available to duly accredited persons.

Effective prosecution of the Council's work requires the cordial collaboration of the scientific and technical branches of the Government, both military and civil. To this end representatives of the Government, upon the nomination of the National Academy of Sciences, will be designated by the President as members of the Council, as heretofore, and the heads of the departments immediately concerned will continue to coöperate in every way that may be required.

(Signed) Woodrow Wilson

The White House
   May 11, 1918

Work of the National Research Council

As pointed out in Dr. Hale's enlightening address, the work of the National Research Council under the President's Executive Order covers such a wide range of subjects as may be imagined between the development and supply of optical glass for periscopes, range-finders, field glasses, and other instruments, to the fixation of atmospheric nitrogen for the manufacture of nitric acid for explosives and for nitrates for other industrial purposes.

In the absence of intensive research of the more fundamental kind, we were caught in the world war, largely dependent upon Germany for optical glass, and upon the nitrate beds of Chile for the fixed nitrogen so necessary for the manufacture of smokeless powder and high explosives.

It was high time we had the " coöperation " and the " coördination " and the organized spirit of research, and the future will without doubt add increased lustre to the saying, " Better late than never."

But the plans for the National Research Council were laid deep and broad, as soon as it was evident that the United States could no longer keep clear of the world conflagration, and on the day preceding the entrance of our country into the war, the following cablegram was sent by Dr. Hale, the Foreign Secretary of the National Academy of Sciences, to

The Royal Society of London,

The Paris Academy of Sciences,

The Accademia dei Lincei of Rome,

The Petrograd Academy of Sciences.

" The entrance of the United States into the

war unites our men of science with yours in a common cause. The National Academy of Sciences, acting through the National Research Council, which has been designated by President Wilson and the Council of National Defense to mobilize the research facilities of the country, would gladly coöperate in any research facilities of the country, would gladly coöperate in any scientific research still underlying the solution of military or industrial problems."

(Signed) Hale,
Foreign Secretary.

Insomuch as the National Research Council has become America's permanent organization for fostering scientific inquiry of the highest order, it may be of interest and value to incorporate here the complete outline of its organization, and also to outline its plan for National Research Fellowships in Physics and Chemistry, supported by the Rockefeller Foundation.

ORGANIZATION OF THE NATIONAL RESEARCH COUNCIL

PREAMBLE

The National Academy of Sciences, under authority conferred upon it by its charter enacted by Congress, and approved by President

Lincoln on March 3, 1863, and pursuant to the request expressed in an Executive Order made by President Wilson on May 11, 1918, hereto appended, adopts the following permanent organization for the National Research Council, to replace the temporary organization under which it has operated heretofore.

Article I. — Purpose

It shall be the purpose of the National Research Council to promote research in the mathematical, physical, and biological sciences, and in the application of these sciences to engineering, agriculture, medicine, and other useful arts, with the object of increasing knowledge, of strengthening the national defense, and of contributing in other ways to the public welfare, as expressed in the Executive Order of May 11, 1918.

Article II. — Membership

Section 1. The membership of the National Research Council shall be chosen with the view of rendering the Council an effective federation of the principal research agencies in the United States concerned with the fields of science and technology named in Article I.

Section 2. The Council shall consist of

1. Representatives of national scientific and technical societies:

2. Representatives of the Government, as provided in the Executive Order:

3. Representatives of other research organizations and other persons whose aid may advance the objects of the Council.

Article III. — Divisions

Section 1. The Council shall be organized in Divisions of two classes:

A. Divisions dealing with the more general relations and activities of the Council;

B. Divisions dealing with related branches of science and technology.

Section 2. The initial constitution of the Divisions of the Council shall be as follows:

A. Divisions of General Relations:

    I. Government Division.

    II. Division of Foreign Relations.

    III. Division of States Relations.

    IV. Division of Educational Relations.

    V. Division of Industrial Relations.

    VI. Research Information Service.

B. Divisions of Science and Technology:

    VII. Division of Physical Sciences.

    VIII. Division of Engineering.

    IX. Division of Chemistry and Chemical Technology.

    X. Division of Geology and Biography.

    XI. Division of Medical Sciences.

    XII. Division of Biology and Agriculture.

XIII. Division of Anthropology and Psychology.

Section 3. The number of divisions and the grouping of subjects in Article III, section 2, may be modified by the Executive Board of the National Research Council.

Section 4. The Divisions of General Relations shall be organized by the Executive Board of the National Research Council (Article IV, section 2).

Section 5. To secure the effective federation of the principal research agencies in the United States, provided for in Article II, a majority of the members of each of the Divisions of Science and Technology shall consist of representatives of scientific and technical societies, chosen as provided for in Article V, section 2. The other members of the Division shall be nominated by the Executive Committee of the Division, approved by the Executive Board of the National Research Council, and appointed in accordance with Article V, section 4.

Section 6. The Divisions of the Council, with the approval of the Executive Board, may establish sections and committees, any of which may include members chosen outside the membership of the Council.

Article IV. — Administration

Section 1. The affairs of each Division shall be administered by a Chairman, a Vice-Chairman, and an Executive Committee, of which the Chairman and the Vice-Chairman shall be ex-officio members; all of whom shall be elected annually by the Division and confirmed by the Executive Board.

Section 2. The affairs of the National Research Council shall be administered by an Executive Board, of which the officers of the Council, the President and Home Secretary of the National Academy of Sciences, the President of the American Association for the Advancement of Science, the Chairmen and Vice-Chairmen of the Divisions of Science and Technology, and the Chairmen of the Divisions of General Relations shall be ex-officio members. The Executive Board may elect additional members, not to exceed ten in number, who, if not already members of the National Research Council, shall be appointed thereto, in accordance with Article V, section 4.

Section 3. The officers of the National Research Council shall consist of a Chairman, one or more Vice-Chairmen, a Secretary, and a Treasurer, who shall also serve as members and officers of the Executive Board of the Council.

Section 4. The officers of the National Research Council, excepting the Treasurer, shall be elected annually by the Executive Board. The Treasurer of the National Academy of Sciences shall be ex-officio Treasurer of the National Research Council.

Section 5. The duties of the officers of the Council and of the Divisions shall be fixed by the Executive Board.

Article V. — Nominations and Appointments

Section 1. The Government bureaus, civil and military, to be represented in the Government Division, and the scientific and technical societies, to be represented in the Divisions of Science and Technology of the National Research Council, shall be determined by joint action of the Council of the National Academy of Sciences and the Executive Board of the National Research Council.

Section 2. Representatives of scientific and technical societies shall be nominated by the societies, at the request of the Executive Board, and appointed by the President of the National Academy of Sciences to membership in the Council and assigned to one of its Divisions.

Section 3. The representatives of the Government shall be nominated by the President of the National Academy of Sciences after conference with the Secretaries of the Departments concerned, and the names of those nominated shall be presented to the President of the United States for designation by him for service with the National Research Council.

Section 4. Other members of the Council shall be nominated by the Executive Committees of the Divisions, approved by the Executive Board, and appointed by the President of the National Academy of Sciences to membership and assigned to one of the Divisions.

Section 5. Prior to the first annual meeting of the Council following January 1, 1919, all Divisions shall be organized by appointment of their members in accordance with Article II and Article V, sections 1 to 4.

Section 6. As far as practicable one-third of the original representatives of each scientific and technical society and approximately one-third of the other original members of each of the Divisions of Science and Technology shall serve for a term of three years; one-third for a term of two years, and one-third for a term of one year, their respective terms to be determined by lot. Each year thereafter, as the terms of members expire, their successors shall be appointed for a period of three years.

Section 7. The Government representatives shall serve for periods of three years, unless they previously retire from the Government office which they represent, in which case their successors shall be appointed for the unexpired term.

Section 8. As far as practicable a similar rotation shall be observed in the appointment of the members of the Divisions of General Relations.

Article VI. — Meetings

Section 1. — The Council shall hold one stated meeting, called the annual meeting, in April of each year, in the city of Washington, on a date to be fixed by the Executive Board. Other meetings of the Council shall be held on call of the Executive Board.

Section 2. The Executive Board and each of the Divisions shall hold an annual meeting, at which officers shall be elected, at the time and place of the annual meeting of the Council, unless otherwise determined by the Executive Board, and such other meetings as may be required for the transaction of business.

Section 3. Joint meetings of the Executive Board of the National Research Council and the Council of the National Academy of Sciences shall be held from time to time, to consider special requests from the Government, the selection of organizations to be represented in the National Research Council, and other matters which, in the judgment of the President of the National Academy, require the attention of both bodies.

Article VII.— Publications and Reports

Section 1. An annual report on the work of the National Research Council shall be presented by the Chairman to the National Academy of Sciences, for submission to Congress in connection with the annual report of the President of the Academy.

Section 2. Other publications of the National Research Council may include papers, bulletins, reports, and memoirs, which may appear in the Proceedings or Memoirs of the National Academy of Sciences, in the publications of other societies, in scientific and technical journals, or in a separate series of the Research Council.

NATIONAL RESEARCH COUNCIL

National Research Fellowships in Physics and Chemistry
Supported by the Rockefeller Foundation

General Statement. —The National Research Council has been entrusted by the Rockefeller Foundation with the expenditure of an appropriation of $500,000, within a period of five years for promoting fundamental research in physics and chemistry primarily in educational institutions of the United States.

The primary feature of the plan is the initiation and maintenance of a system of National Research Fellowships, which are to be awarded by the National Research Council to persons who have demonstrated a high order of ability in research, for the purpose of enabling them to conduct investigations at educational institutions which make adequate provision for effective prosecution of research in physics or chemistry. The plan will include such supplementary features as may promote its broad purpose and increase its efficiency.

Purposes in View. — Among the important results which are expected to follow from the execution of the plan may be mentioned:

(1) Opening of a scientific career to a larger number of able investigators and their more thorough training in research, thus meeting an urgent need of our universities and industries.

(2) Increase of knowledge relating to the fundamental principles of physics and chemistry, upon which the progress of all the sciences and the development of industry depend.

(3) Creation of more favorable conditions for research in the educational institutions of this country.

Administration. — The plan will be administered by the Research Fellowship Board of the National Research Council. This Board consists of six members appointed for terms of five years, and of the chairmen ex-officiis of the Division of Physical Science and the Division of Chemistry and Chemical Technology of the National Research Council. The members of the Board are:

Henry A. Bumstead, Professor of Physics, Yale University.

Simon Flexner, Director of Laboratories, Rockefeller Institution for Medical Research.

George E. Hale, Director of Mount Wilson Observatory.

Elmer P. Kohler, Professor of Chemistry, Harvard University.

Robert A. Millikan, Professor of Physics, University of Chicago.

Arthur A. Noyes, Director of the Research Laboratory of Physical Chemistry, Massachusetts Institute of Technology.

Wilder D. Bancroft, Professor of Physical Chemistry, Cornell University.

Chairman of the Division of Chemistry and Chemical Technology.

Chairman of the Division of Physical Science.

Coöperations of Educational Institutions. — National Research Fellows will be permitted to conduct their investigations at institutions that will coöperate in meeting their needs. These needs differ widely from those of students seeking only instruction. Able investigators, actively engaged in productive research, are needed to inspire and guide the work of the Fellows. Research laboratories, adequately manned with assistants and mechanicians, and amply supplied with instruments, machine tools, and other facilities, are indispensable; and funds to provide supplies and to satisfy the constantly recurrent demands of research must be available. Above all, there must exist the stimulating atmosphere found only in institutions that have brought together a group of men devoted to the advancement of science through pursuit of research.

The Research Fellowship Board expects to make arrangements by which educational institutions will associate the Research Fellows with their graduate departments and offer the most favorable conditions for the prosecution of their researches.

The applicant will indicate one or more institutions at which, in his opinion, his research work can be conducted to the best advantage.

Fellowship Appointments. — The appointments of National Research Fellows will be made only after careful consideration of the scientific attainments of all candidates, not only of those who apply on their own initiative, but also of those who are brought to the attention of the Fellowship Board by professors in educational institutions and by other investigators throughout the country. In making the appointments much weight will also be given to the judgment shown by the applicant in selecting and planning his proposed research.

The Research Fellowships will for the most part be awarded to American citizens who have had training equivalent to that represented by the Doctor's degree. The salary will ordinarily be $1500 for the first year. The Research Fellowship Board will not, however, be bound by rigid rules of procedure. Thus it may offer larger salaries to those of exceptional attainment or wider experience, and may give appointment to competent investigators who have had training other than that represented by the Doctor's degree. The Research Fellows will be appointed for one year; but they will be eligible for successive reappointments, ordinarily with increase of salary.

Fellowship Regulations. — Research Fellows are expected to devote their entire time to research, except that during the college year they may at their option give not more than one-fifth of their time (outside preparation included) to teaching of educational value to themselves, or to attendance on advanced courses of study. They may associate graduate students with their researches. They shall not engage in work for remuneration during the term of their appointment. Fellows who have not received the Doctor's degree may, with the approval of the institution, offer their research work in partial fulfillment of the requirements for that degree.

Fellows are expected to submit to the Board shortly before the first of April of each year a detailed report on the progress of their researches. They must also present an account of their researches in form for publication before withdrawing from the Fellowship; and final salary payments will be deferred until this condition is fulfilled. It is understood that all results of investigation by the Fellows shall be made available to the public without restriction.

Fellowship appointments are subject to the condition that after they are accepted by the applicant, they will not be vacated within the year without consent of the Research Fellowship Board.

Fellowship Applications. —It is expected that fifteen to twenty Research Fellowships will be available during the coming year, and that the number will be increased in subsequent years. Applications for these Fellowships should be made on the form provided for the purpose, and should be sent to the Secretary of the Research Fellowship Board, National Research Council, 1023 Sixteenth Street, Washington, D.C., to whom all other correspondence should also be addressed. Applications will be re-

CHAPTER V

The Education for Research

LORD KELVIN, the Great English physicist and illustrious research worker, said that the first object of technical education was "to enable a man to live," and that the second object was "to assist others to live."

As a nation must first be prepared for war, before it can secure its actual army and navy, so with the successful research worker and inventor; he must first be suitably equipped, before he is competent to attack the bigger problems in physics, chemistry and engineering, or wrestle effectually with the great secrets of nature in general.

So it should be fully appreciated that education applies fundamentally to nations, which are but aggressions of men; for to enable a nation to live, to live fully and richly, economically, safely, soundly and sanely, education is of the first importance.

Germany, as has been seen, was a most highly educated nation, but one woefully unbalanced in her conceptions. Like the imposed burden of dead languages and their literature and the useless frills of higher mathematics upon the average bread-winning individual in certain of our colleges, she as a nation went insane with *military instruction*, and the autocrats in power warped her to her destruction.

Plato, for example, was in a sense like the German Kaiser, an intellectual aristocrat, but with a rich and fertile imagination. He favored the education of the directing classes *only*, men trained in his own false philosophical and ethical conceptions, and his stupid and selfish influence was very far reaching. It was Plato who placed the teaching of mathematics in the first place of the sciences, for over his academy at Athens, it will be remembered, he placed the famous inscription, *Medeis agometretes eisito*, which translated means: "Let no one ignorant of geometry enter here."

Plato was born in the year 429 B.C., and along with his philosophy of educating only the directing classes and the aristocracy, his moral philosophy was based upon abstract thought, mental purity, unaccompanied by any sensuous emotions between two persons of the opposite sex, and the practice of the strictest morality. "We immoralists," wrote Nietzsche, on the other hand, in his "Will to Power," "we are the most advanced," and his teachings were more rational and unselfish, for he believed in a pure democracy of education. In the place of "Equal and inalienable rights to life, liberty and the pursuit of happiness," he advanced the very significant idea of scaling all men according to their actual worth to the community. He proposed an unalloyed merit plan of democracy, based solely upon education, achievement and ability to construct; and with the promised bombardment of the idle rich today, we may look for, I think, some modern materialization and developments from this old immoralist.

This merit plan of democracy, although modified, has been actually in vogue in China, and upon education and achievement, there, is based the Mandarin's rank; but the scheme was, after all, not a pure democracy of wisdom, for to compete in the examinations which were held at Canton and Nanking and other important Chinese cities, a candidate had to present a certificate setting forth the importance of his family from the *social* point of view.

The examinations were barred, for example, to barbers, actors, and boatmen, and to men occupied with certain other vocations.

Another example in the form of a very amusing attempt at educational limitation, which dates back to Alexander the Great, is given here to illustrate greedy selfishness.

Among the principal physical treatises of Aristotle, it may be remembered, are the eight famous books of his " Physical Lectures," which are undoubtedly the works concerning which the interesting story is told by Simplicus, a Greek commentator of the Sixth Century.

As the story goes, Alexander the Great wrote to Aristotle, who was his former instructor, and said: "You have not done well in publishing these lectures; for how shall we, your pupils, excel other men, if you make that public to all, which we learned from you?" Aristotle is said to have replied: "My lectures are published and not published; they will be intelligible to those who heard them, and to none others."

The spirit of selfishness as shown by Alexander the Great, if the story be true, and I have no doubt of it, is fortunately not in vogue today in America, where *general* knowledge and great fundamental principles of science are concerned, but precious little effort, if any, has been made to educate the inventor in research efficiency, and to show him the proper ropes, and steer him clear of the many false and misleading structures.

We are fortunately not in Germany or China today, and there should be no obstacles whatever to an ideally pure democracy of education for the fruits of research and discovery in America, and when this is duly appreciated, the efficiency of productiveness will without doubt enormously increase. Self-made men, who have lived with fame acquired by revealing the secrets of nature, or in contriving ingenious new devices and processes, have, as has already been pointed out, been quite numerous in America for a hundred years.

Where one man has succeeded and succeeds, however, in the fairyland of research, tens of thousands fail, and I am convinced from an analysis of many cases that have come under my immediate notice, that this failure ofttimes is due wholly to preventable reasons. Among these preventable reasons, lack of education is the chief cause, and by education in this connection, is not meant wholly book learning, with its theoretical training value and accompanying capacity for getting free from the structure of false science, but in knowing how to proceed economically in the practical development of a research, an invention or a process, and in keeping clear of snares and pitfalls, as well as wild goose chases. Some reading knowledge of the history and prior art of the subject is, therefore, manifestly essential in the educational equipment. A few days spent in library research as a preliminary to an actual instrumental research may save weeks or months, or even years, of unhappy toil. I cannot too strongly impress the importance of a library prior art survey upon the mind of the reader here. No better investment of time could be made.

There has, to a very great extent, as already

suggested, been a monopoly in American research by those keen to the requirements, and especially fitted, and who know the secret ropes, instead of a democracy of research, in spite of the many brilliant flights of Yankee fancy which are already on record.

The commonwealth of pure and applied science should, of course, be democratic to the highest degree, and we should lose no time in searching for the underlying secrets to success and attempting to remedy all factors which tend toward limitations.

There is, therefore, urgent need for technical research education, because now that the war is over there will continue a still fiercer war of competition in the years to come for supremacy in the arts and sciences.

The art of economic research and invention should, therefore, without delay, be regarded as a serious and leading profession, and one should choose his subjects in the future, just as one does when he specializes for success in medicine, authorship, shipbuilding, or engineering, and the great natural psychological forces and passions at work should be directed along economic lines. Like the great water-powers which are now going to waste in many parts of the nation, productive thought is likewise to a great extent flowing, non-productive, through uneconomic races.

And in connection with educational efficiency, is not the true education of a young man, after all, based largely upon the teaching of a spirit of inquiry, and is not this attitude one of research and inquiry?

It is, of course, not meant that all youth be taught the spirit of contrivance, speaking strictly from the *mechanical* point of view, but invention in the broadest sense, to enable him to meet life's flow of problems with a *ready method* as to their solution.

The trite saying that necessity is the mother of invention is very forcefully illustrated in the lives of young men on the farm lands, for it has been pointed out that the sons of farmers often excel when engaged in later years in industrial life, because in their country living it has been said that " Every hillside, every roadway, every gully, every new rainfall, every changing season, every unmanageable beast, presents a new problem which to a greater or less extent has to be solved by the farmer's son unaided." This country boy, brought up in contact with hard practical work, and in a sense with " bread and butter " studies, is more apt, and ready, as to *method* in meeting the problems of life, than he of the city, laden with the time-honored classics, embracing the two dead languages and their literature, for which he may have no liking, and the usual impractical higher

LEO HENDRIK BAEKELAND

Chemist, Inventor of "Velox" and "Bakelite."

Born at Ghent, Belgium, Nov. 14th, 1863. B.S. University of Ghent, 1882, Sc.D. 1884. Laureate of the four Belgian Universities. Ch.D. University of Pittsburg, 1916. Assistant, and later Associate Professor of Chemistry, University of Ghent, 1882 to 1889. Professor of Chemistry and Physics, Government Higher Normal School of Science, Bruges, Belgium 1885 to 1889.

Came to America in 1889; founded, 1893, and conducted until 1899, Nepera Chemical Company, manufacturers of photographic papers (Velox Paper, etc.), and since in research chemical work.

President General Bakelite Company, manufacturers of Bakelite (a chemical synthesis from carbolic acid and formaldehyde, replacing hard rubber and amber).

Member Naval Consulting Board, 1915 —; Member Nitrate Supply Committee of National Research Council. Awarded Nichols Medal, American Chemical Society, 1909; Willard Gibbs Medal, American Chemical Society, Chicago Section, 1913; Chandler Medal (first award), Columbia University, 1914. Perkin Medal for Industrial Chemical Research, 1916; Grand Prize, Panama Pacific Exposition, 1915. Now Honorary Professor of Chemical Engineering, Columbia University. President Inventor's Guild, 1914. President of American Institute of Chemical Engineers, 1912; President Section of Plastics, International Congress of Chemistry, 1912.

Member of American Chemical Society, Vice President, 1909, Chairman New York Section, 1908, Councilor at Large, 1907–; American Electro-chemical Society, President, 1909; Society of Chemical Industry, Vice President, 1905; Member Naval Consulting Board, 1915.

mathematics. Perhaps the fundamental difference between the practical inventive work of the country boy and the theoretical curriculum, along which the city boy is induced in his studies, may be roughly expressed as the difference between teaching the power of thought and the power of memory. No one will deny, I am sure, that it is preferable to know a little by reason, than much by rote.

Of course we must not lose sight of the fact that some few minds have a powerful penchant for the things and lessons of the past, and that we should recognize and carefully classify the types of minds as early as possible in order that they may not be artificially directed along wrong channels.

"Among all the movements of thought," writes F. Hodson, "the first was the classical renaissance: the second the study of natural science. Each has worked in the main upon different materials, the one upon the texts and monuments of antiquity, the other upon nature closely scrutinized and comprehensively observed."

Let us have no objection whatever to the renaissance or other culture studies for the type of mind that is found to crave them, and let us have no objection to adding to these culture studies certain of the fancy frills of higher mathematics.

Dr. G. W. Thompson writes in this connection: " I believe that our universities and colleges should, all of them, turn more to the practical aspects of education. Many of them think only of its cultural side. Culture is desirable; no one questions this; but culture is not incompatible with an education that suits a man for the practical affairs of life."

It is customary to point out how very accurate one becomes who is trained in the higher mathematics, and I will concede that some, of course, excel in this connection, but on the other hand, many become as primly precise and impractically accurate as the illustrious old mathematician who owned a cat and a kitten. This old fellow was so exact that he is said to have cut a large hole in his fence, through which the cat could go to and fro, and then he cut a small hole, in order that the kitten might follow its mother in her little excursions.

In attacking the often unnecessary teaching of the higher mathematics, and the real lack of practical use to the great majority of those who have studied them in after life, I am fully aware that its advocates always bring up the hackneyed battery of arguments of precise mental training; but I shall attack what I believe to be the wasteful and overdone teaching of higher mathematics, nevertheless, because I am certain that there are other sciences far more valuable to the research worker and inventor, and equally valuable, if not infinitely more so, in mental training.

Mathematics has been called the most important tool of the engineer, and my only plea is to keep the tool a practical one, and not a fancy plaything taught at the expense of more deserving subjects. Opinions differ as to the wisest methods of teaching mathematics. Sub-committee IX of the International Commission on the Teaching of Mathematics reports "that it appears that mathematics teachers are generally agreed that mathematics should be taught as a science by professional mathematicians, and not as a tool by engineers." This is, of course, all right if the professional mathematicians do not lose their heads and overdo it by insisting on teaching the poor engineer to blow, so to speak, all kinds of useless fancy rings of smoke. While the study of advanced mathematics quickens a very useful type of intelligence, it does not necessarily develop resourcefulness or self-reliance except on paper.

It is often a boast that our Naval Academy and many of our engineering schools are based upon a wonderful mathematical curriculum, but just for fun, let the reader sometime test out an Annapolis graduate or an engineer after he has been away from the academy or his engineering school for a few years or even a few months, and it will be found that this Annapolis graduate or the engineer has considerable difficulty in using his mathematics as a rough and ready tool. He will, however, remember, to a large degree, his working principles of chemistry and physics, his practical foundations of navigation and engineering and the more concrete things and be very hazy on the abstractions he learned. I asked a well-known mechanical engineer very recently if he remembered his calculus. Let me quote his reply: " Oh, the Devil, no! " he said.

Should I be overstrenuous in my protest against the continued persistence in the teaching of unnecessary mathematics, it may be due in part to the fact that one of my mathematical professors said when I was a student in the university, " that I would never make an engineer or be successful in original research because I did not know mathematics enough."

I have managed to hobble along with my old slide-rule and pocketbooks of physical and chemical data, and I do not expect to change my tactics in the future. I did not like mathematics and I was loath to be absorbed by its abstraction to the necessary exclusion of other subjects I loved best. It has too often come under my notice that a fellow with a natural passion for creative work will become discouraged when he looks through text-books with the pages all covered with mathematical idiosyncrasies and say: "It is all beyond me, I do not feel that I can ever succeed." He becomes disheartened in his reading, and the rich field of experimental research very often loses many good men to work it through this cause.

But there is a great field also for the mathematically inclined. Let them specialize in it as a language, for a complex language it is, with its rules, its grammar, and its signs and symbols. The specialist in mathematics becomes proficient in expressing through formulae and equations verbally stated facts in this condensed mathematical language, but its value as a working tool depends absolutely upon the great foundation of the laboratory and its deductive methods. Let the mathematically inclined specialize and come in for conferences when essential. I have called these fellows in quite frequently in my engineering work to help out my old slide-rule, but up to the present writing with only fair success. A distinguished consulting steam engineer, a friend of mine, recently sought data on the static and dynamic balance of a turbine rotor and shaft. These rotors and shafts have various vibratory periods in their performance and go through nodes and harmonics at the different speeds at which they are driven. My friend had a famous mathematician work out the dynamic balance and when the machine was put into operation the maximum racking vibration took place at the normal operating speed! Nothing could have been worse. Mathematicians had it conclusively demonstrated that mechanical flight was impossible and the helicopter, with its vertical shaft and horizontally operated propellers, conformed to their abstractions by proving a failure. But all of the wise mathematician's endeavor was completely upset by the simple little trick of turning the vertical shaft with its horizontal propellers into a horizontal shaft with vertical propellers and equipping the machine with planes.

Dr. Charles P. Steinmetz, one of the ablest mathematicians and electrical engineers today, told me recently during a friendly discussion of the value of mathematics, that the steamer *Persia* in 1832 brought over to America in the mail a mathematical calculation setting forth the impossibility of a coal-burning steamer to cross the Atlantic! Of course mathematicians will claim that the physical constants were in error, and I suppose in this instance some of them were.

Enough experimental deductive work had evidently not been done to construct the formulae. I take the position that the two great basic sciences of physics and chemistry *originated experimentally in the laboratory* and that deductive work is the most basic and vital and by far the most fertile field for the great majority who read these lines.

But enough of mathematics. Let us now try to set down an ideal mental equipment for those without the benefit of a college education as projected by an analysis of the governing conditions, and endeavor to fill in the gaps, so to speak, wherever in the light of them we may consider ourselves deficient.

The foundation of the practical inventor and research worker should most naturally consist of a good working knowledge of the principles of chemistry and physics, sufficient mathematics, possibly limited to advanced arithmetic, and enough manual training to give him " the feel of the machines and tools " with which he deals.

Professor Thorndike made practical tests on the Freshmen in an engineering school:

" Out of one hundred and three engineering Freshmen who reported on the matter of boyish activities, writes Dr. Charles Riborg Mann, in his splendid ' Study of Engineering Education,' ninety-one had constructed on their own initiative mechanical or scientific devices, such as cannon, telegraph lines, telephones, electric motors, arc lights, gasoline motors, lathe, steam engine, water wheels, boats, etc. None of the engineering schools at present record this type of information, or make any systematic effort to use it or to interpret its meaning: nor do parents and elementary school teachers realize the importance of giving young boys and girls opportunities of expressing their innate mechanical sense in creative work."

In order to discover such tendencies and to develop them, Dean Schneider, at the University of Cincinnati in 1906, found an opportunity to make an interesting educational experiment:

" The mechanism of the scheme is very simple. The students are divided into two groups, one of which is assigned to work in industrial plants, while the other goes to school. At the end of each bi-weekly period, the two groups change places, so that the shops and the schools are always well manned. In the shops the students work as regular workmen for pay, but the nature of their work and the length of time each stays on any particular job are subject to approval by the University. The emphasis of the school work is on the theory and principles, but these are well interrelated with the shop-work by ' coördinators,' who visit each student during each shop period and then meet the several groups during the university periods in special 'coödination' classes for this purpose."

Dr. Henry S. Pritchett, President of the Carnegie Foundation for the Advancement of Teaching, in a most interesting manner compares Langdell's method of teaching law with the methods in vogue in teaching science. " Langdell," writes Dr. Pritchett:

" built the teaching of law exclusively and directly upon the study of cases. His notion was that the principles upon which the law rests are few in number, and that these could be best apprehended and mastered by the student in the direct examination of typical cases. The number of such cases necessary to illustrate these principles he held to be very small in comparison with the overwhelming mass of law reports to which the student had formerly been directed as the basis of the study of the law in conjunction with textbooks. Langdell's method involved the working out by the student of the principles of the law from actual cases tried and decided in the courts. Law he conceived of as an Applied Science. . . . Applied Science is not taught ordinarily in the engineering school by the case method. On the contrary, the methods actually employed in teaching the so-called laboratory subjects do not differ appreciably from the methods of teaching literature or Latin. At present the student undertakes to learn a vast body of theory under the name of physics, mechanics, or chemistry, illustrated in some measure in the laboratory, and then seeks later to select from this mass of knowledge the principles to be applied, for example, in electrical engineering. The case method would proceed in directly the opposite manner. Taking up, for example, the dynamo as a ' case,'— that is, as an illustration of physical laws in their actual concrete working, — it would proceed to analyze the machine for the purpose of discovering the fundamental physical or mechanical principles involved in its operation. It would lead the student from practical applications by analogies to a comprehension of theory, instead of from theory to applications as under present methods of teaching."

But let us return to our chemistry and physics, as the basic sciences for the research worker and inventor, and let us examine these subjects to see what they really comprise.

Chemistry may be split up into: 1. Inorganic Chemistry, the study of the metals and non-carbon compounds. 2. Organic Chemistry, the study of the carbon compounds. 3. Physical Chemistry, that branch which takes note of energy changes as well as chemical changes within the molecules. 4. Electrochemistry, the applications of the electric current to chemistry. 5. Industrial Chemistry, or chemical engineering, which consists of the great superstructure resting upon the foundations of the branches just enumerated. Of course each one of these subjects may be divided into many subheadings and these subheadings may again be divided down to the ultimate analysis.

As to physics we may divide this great subject into: 1. Mechanics, 2. Light, 3. Heat, 4. Sound, 5. Electricity, 6. Magnetism, with a still greater superstructure which may be called mechanical and electrical engineering.

In the teaching of all of these subjects, actual

contact with practical *things* is, as has already been pointed out, absolutely essential to successful research. " I think that the sickliest notion of physics, even if a student gets it," writes W. S. Franklin, " is that it is the science of masses, molecules and the ether." And I think that the healthiest notion, even if a student does not wholly get it, is that physics is the science of the ways of taking hold of bodies and pushing them; that it is the aggregate of all things that can be " by handling known."

Let the young man or young woman who may read and heed these suggestions guard also against premature *theoretical* specialization and thereby keep as free as possible in a neutral field, if it may be so expressed, in order to be capable of using principles and phenomena at will from the several great sciences.

The student with this groundwork, and enough of the three R's — reading, writing and arithmetic — should also possess a good slide-rule, pocket-books, self-reliance, a persistency which is often a ruling passion, resourcefulness and an opportunity to come into contact with practical things and problems in his fields of activity. The student with a rich and active imagination in addition to these requisites, and with powers to rise to the full height of his imagination, is almost sure to succeed. But the objector will say that many of the books dealing with the enumerated subjects cannot be read and understood by anyone, especially by those without mathematical knowledge. Do not let this discourage. It has been said that " it took a quarter of a century for anyone to comprehend what Gibbs had written." And when " Arrhenius had his electrolytic dissociation theory perfectly clear to himself, he admits that he did not dare include it in his doctor's thesis, for fear he would thereby lose the hope for doctor's degree." My suggestion is to get the books, and there are fortunately many of them dealing with all subjects in simple and straightforward language. If you don't understand a subject as presented by an author in a book, get another book by another author, and perhaps this other author will have an entirely different light, illuminating more clearly the difficult subject. " I think that the ability to learn science by reading is a highly specialized faculty," continues W. S. Franklin, " and that among average young men this faculty is nearly zero. I know many men who are quick to receive knowledge by experience, and quick to catch, by verbal description, manifold variations of their empirical knowledge, but whose imagination is wholly unresponsive to that abstract kind of writing which is necessary in a concise treatise on the elements of physics." " Nevertheless, I think that it is necessary to enable him to follow concise writing as one of the chief objects in the teaching of physics and I do not believe that this result can be accomplished without requiring the student to use a text-book of the severest kind."

The advice up to the present has been cast by the author primarily for the industriously inclined who have not been able to secure a technical school or university education. In concluding the present chapter some data should be given upon the methods in vogue in the technical schools of the country, and the able studies that are being conducted to increase their efficiency.

In connection with the systematic and comprehensive study of American engineering schools, Dr. Charles Riborg Mann writes:

" Since engineering is perhaps the most objective of all professions, it offers excellent opportunities for the scientific study of objective tests. A study of engineering education, therefore, provides an appropriate opportunity to initiate experiments and to attempt to sort out the more promising methods of investigation from those that prove to be less fruitful."

To this end Professor Edward L. Thorndike of Columbia University undertook a special series of experiments with Freshmen in engineering at Columbia, Massachusetts Institute of Technology, the University of Cincinnati, and Wentworth Institute.

The experiences with the Columbia group are here described as typical of the principles and methods applied:

". . . Through the courtesy of Dean F. P. Keppel, an invitation was extended by Professor Thorndike to forty Freshmen in engineering to spend two successive Saturdays (fourteen hours) in taking the tests. Each of the thirty-four students who completed the series was given a small fee and a full statement of his record. Fifteen tests in all were used, each designed to record the student's relative ability in some one particular activity which was complete in itself, altho it involved a rather complicated series of reactions. Thus each student was asked to read paragraphs and write answers to questions on their meaning, to identify words as proof of his range of vocabulary, to supply missing words in sentences, to solve arithmetical and algebraic problems, to perform algebraic computations, to draw graphs from given data, to give geometrical proofs of stated theorems, to solve problems in physics described in words, to arrange apparatus to secure stated results, to match each of a series of pictures with one of a series of verbal statements, to supply missing lines in drawings of machinery, and to construct simple mechanical devices from their unassembled parts."

This experimental work appears to the author to be a firm and active step forward in the right direction, emphasizing less mathematical abstractions and more contact with concrete things, and this type of training and development should be applied perhaps in a more strenuous and advanced scheme also to the instructor.

Professor James Swinburne in a lecture on Science and Industry delivered recently in King's College, England, points out, as have others in France and Germany, that limitations to abstraction and theory exist to a great extent with the instructors and professors in technology, and with our own collegiate staffs in technology, many are out of touch with practical conditions, but with more of the worth of the academician.

It has been said on the other hand that it is impractical to attempt to teach research in education and to secure any definite results in the impersonal measurement of the vaguely defined and illusive qualities of human beings. As Dr. Mann points out: " The fact that such measurements have as yet been rather crude and inconclusive is no reason against trying to improve them."

Let me illustrate much that has been said with a single comparison of mathematical abstraction versus concrete objective in mental training.

Here are three of the mathematical abstractions I studied in college:

What is the chance of throwing at least two sixes in 6 throws with a die?

I remember the answer was $\dfrac{12281}{46656}$.

Would you bank your pocketbook on it? No? Neither would I!

Here is another — From 7 Englishmen and 4 Americans, a committee of 6 is to be formed, containing 2 Americans; in how many ways can this be done?

Here we have to choose 2 Americans out of 4, and 4 Englishmen out of 7. The number of ways in which the Americans can be chosen is 4^c2; and the number of ways in which the Englishmen can be chosen is 7^c4. Each of the first groups can be associated with each of the second. Hence the required number of ways is

$$4^c2 \times 7^c4 = \frac{\lfloor 14}{\lfloor 2 \lfloor 2} \times \frac{\lfloor 7}{\lfloor 4 \lfloor 3} - \frac{\lfloor 7}{\lfloor 2 \lfloor 2 \lfloor 3} = 210.$$

This may all be fine, but which of the 210 committees would be the best? Would we be able to say that any of them would be worth a hang unless we had deductive knowledge of the men themselves by actual contact? Again I had:

A man and his wife could drink a cask of beer in 20 days, the man drinking half as much again as his wife; but $\dfrac{18}{25}$ of a gallon having leaked

away, they found that it only lasted them together for 18 days, and the wife herself for two
days longer. How much did the cask contain
when full?

The answer is 12 gallons. Can you picture
in real life a man and his better half sitting down
and drinking a keg of beer in such a manner,
especially for a woman to out-drink her husband?
How did they measure the $\frac{18}{25}$ of a gallon leak-

age? It was an extremely irritating problem.

Here is a concrete objective and to my mind
a far more beautiful thing to think out, a practical example in concise writing based upon
scientific facts. I believe the thinking out and
the exposition of some such physical principle
is just as valuable, if not more so, in mental
training than mathematical abstraction. It is
a new balance.

"The new balance is described by the inventors, Professor E. D. Steele and Mr. Kerr
Grant, in the Proceedings of the Royal Society
for 1909, and in addition to the interest attach-
ing to the application of the fundamental idea
involved, a balance of this construction, with
some modifications in detail, was used by Professor Sir William Ramsay and Dr. R. Whytlaw
Gray in determining the density of the gaseous
emanation from radium (q.v.), which Ramsay
calls ' niton.'

" The rationale of the method of weighing is as follows: If a bulb filled with air is at the same temperature and pressure as the air surrounding it, the weight of the contained air will be nothing. This is in accordance with the principle of Archimedes.

"If, however, the pressure of the air surrounding the bulb is altered, the sealed-up air exerts more or less of its full weight. By suspending a bulb containing a known quantity of air at one arm of a balance, and arranging the whole instrument within a case from which the air can be pumped out to any desired extent, the effective weight of the bulb of air can be changed to any amount desired.

" Temperature changes are eliminated as far as possible, as well as vibration, by mounting the balance on a stone pillar in a cellar, and placing the brass case of the balance inside a large box of bright tin plate. The above diagram will give an idea of the essential parts of the micro-balance of Steele and Grant.

" A is the beam of the balance constructed in the form of two triangles base to base, and made of fused quartz rod, 0.6 millimeter in diameter; the whole weighing less than half a gram. The frame thus formed oscillates about a central knife edge, ground at the end of the vertical rod, and resting on a plane quartz plate F. Attached to this beam at its center

c. The weight of this suspended system is always adjusted to equilibrate the counterpoise attached to the opposite end of the balance.

" The method of weighing is as follows: if the quantity of substance to be weighed does not exceed the total weight of the air contained in the bulb, the pressure inside the balance case and the resting point having been taken with the scale pan empty, the substance to be weighed is placed on the pan and the pressure adjusted till the same resting point is obtained.

" If w is the total weight of air contained in the bulb, which was filled at pressure P, and P' represents the difference in pressure required to recover the original resting point, then the weight of the substance is wP'/P. If the quantity of substance to be weighed exceeds the weight of air contained in the bulb it is necessary to prepare one or more counterpoises which must be lighter than the original counterpoise c, and must differ from each other by a known amount not exceeding w.

" The resting or zero point of the instrument is found by the position taken by the image of a Nernst lamp reflected from the mirror attached to the beam. The case is deprived of air by means of a vacuum pump connected through the two-way stopcock x, and the pressure of the residual air is determined by observing the height of the mercury column in the manometer, which is read by means of a telescope and scale to a tenth of a millimeter.

"The attachments for the release of the beam consist of two V-shaped quartz rods which just center the beam but do not lift it. These can be lowered when required by means of the curved brass wire, g, connected as shown in the figure with the upright brass support. The wire is controlled by an excentric cam, o, rotated by a handle passing air-tight through a plug in the side of the case.

"Such a description as the foregoing is only capable of giving an idea of the way in which the pneumatic principle is applied to the determination of weight. As to the possibilities of such a balance the statement of the authors is as follows: 'Weights of the order of one-hundredth of a milligramme may be compared with the standard measures with an accuracy of one five-hundredth of their amounts, $i.e.$, the absolute value of such weights can be determined with certainty to one fifty-thousandth of a milligramme (2×10^{-8} gramme), while changes of weight can be measured of an order as low as one two-hundred-and-fifty-thousandth of a milligramme.'

"With such appliances the mote in the sunbeam becomes a ponderable mass!"

As stated at the outset, this comparison between an abstraction and a concrete piece of apparatus dealing with fundamental physical constants is but an example to illustrate the point that mental training may be secured at the time that a keen insight is gained into the facts and forces of nature. Of course, such examples could be endlessly multiplied, but such elaborations would be out of place here, since the reader may secure all of the material of this character which he may need in the scores of able and practical non-mathematical textbooks dealing with natural philosophy.

I am frequently asked if one can become an engineer or an expert researcher without a university education, and wherever I have the opportunity of advising in this connection, I have been accustomed to take the safe course and advise if practicable to pursue a university education. In giving this advice I fully realize that many brilliant minds have succeeded and developed phenomenal initiative outside of the university curriculum, and had they pursued a rigid university course it is a question whether much of their initiative would not have been stunted or destroyed. But I believe with such experiments upon college students as have been briefly described in the foregoing pages, that the university engineering courses in the future will be shaped much more to conform with the practical and research type of mind.

In connection with the question as to whether

or no a young man or a young woman should secure a university education, I can do no better than reflect the views here of the late President Gilman of Johns Hopkins University, who wrote:

" Nobody can tell how it comes to pass that men of extraordinary minds are born of commonplace parentage and bred in schools of adversity, away from books and masters. Institutions are not essential to their education. But everyone who observes in a series of years the advancement of men of talents, as distinguished from men of genius, must believe that the fostering diet of the university — its plain living and high thinking — favor the growth of scholars, investigators, reasoners, statesmen of enduring reputation, poets and discoverers. Such men are rarely produced in the freedom of the wilderness, in the publicity of travel or trade, or in the seclusion of private life; they are not the natural product of libraries and museums when these stand apart from universities, they are rarely produced by schools of the lower grade."

And in concluding this chapter a few words on the subject of graduate instruction may not be amiss. It appears to be the tendency of technical and engineering scholars to recognize that certain types of students should without question pursue one or two additional years of special study — in fact it has been suggested that the serious and intensive types of workers be collected near the end of their fourth year at college and be either given a scholarship or be substantially assisted in securing the ways and means to pursue their graduate studies.

The Society for the Promotion of Engineering Education has been, and is still, doing work of a most valuable nature in connection with the molding of university courses. At one of its recent meetings it invited the American Society of Civil Engineers, the American Society of Mechanical Engineers, the American Institute of Chemical Engineers, and the American Chemical Society to appoint delegates to the Society for the Promotion of Engineering Education, thereby forming a joint committee on engineering education and engineering research as taught in the undergraduate and graduate schools of the country. This committee invited the Carnegie Foundation for the Advancement of Teaching to take part in the work, which it has done in a very handsome manner, and the result of its coöperation has recently been published in its Bulletin #11, by Professor Charles Riborg Mann.

In selecting an institution for graduate study it is, of course, rational to select the university with a reputation for strength in the particular line of activity in which the student intends to specialize. "In the realm of physics," writes Dr. Richard C. Maclaurin, president of the

CHAPTER VI

Some Borderline Limits

THE present chapter is written primarily for the benefit of skeptics, and especially is it addressed to those who, in the light of the world's phenomenal progress in science, still cling as it were to the old-fashioned conservatism.

We used to express ourselves very freely as to the possibility of this, or the impossibility of that, but it takes a brave man today, if he has any reputation at all to lose, to come out into the open and say it cannot be done.

> " The man who once most wisely said,
>   ' Be sure you're right, then go ahead,'
>   Might well have added this, to wit:
>   ' Be sure you're wrong before you quit.' "

Let us consider some old-fashioned borderline limits in connection with a few accomplished facts, and for the first illustration the art of mechanical flight furnishes a most typical case.

The great Lord Kelvin, one of the profoundest mathematical physicists that ever lived, wrote in 1896 to Colonel Baden Powell — " I have not the *smallest molecule* of faith in aerial navigation other than ballooning, or of expectation of good results from any of the trials we hear of. So you will understand that I would not care to be a member of the aeronautical society."

Just to think that a mind as keen as Kelvin's should have been duped by pseudo borderline barriers, and that other great scientists followed closely in his footsteps.

Le Conte, the illustrious geologist, is blamed for his skeptical remarks in retarding the realization of mechanical flight, for it was his stupid theory that no machine could exceed in size the largest of his fossil birds!

All the way down through the annals of history, including Darius Green and his flying machine, through the unhappy time when the American newspapers and the people ridiculed dear old Professor Langley into his grave just as he was making his master strokes which have immortalized his name, " everybody was expert, — poets and mechanics, bible students and governments."

And perhaps it is proper in this connection to suggest to the reader to avoid this word "expert." I have always steered clear of it and its pompous atmosphere, and I try to avoid it even when testifying in court in technical cases, in making expositions of prior art or in giving my opinions. I like nothing better than to lie in wait to put scientific questions to the pompous type who claims with all self-assurance to be an expert.

But let us return and look a little further into this matter of experts and mechanical flight. The renowned Hiram Maxim said — " I think we may, therefore, conclude that, as far as balloons are concerned, it would not be possible to improve greatly upon what Mr. Santos Dumont has already accomplished." Hiram Maxim also said — " In all nature, we do not find a single balloon, and nature has not yet developed a bird that can fly on petroleum." Santos Dumont, it will be remembered, could navigate the air in fair weather, and with his machinery drive the balloon against a moderate breeze, but the question has been asked if you could really blame a Zeppelin commander on a thousand-mile war raid carrying a ton or more of high explosives during teacherous winter weather, for dropping it upon Mr. Hiram Maxim's English experiment station?

Our own great American mathematician, Simon Newcomb, when professor of mathematics at the United States Naval Academy, wrote — " All should admit that if any hope for the flying machine can be entertained, it must be based more on general faith in what mankind is going to do than upon either reasoning or experience. . . . But, as I have already intimated, there is another great fact of progress which should limit this hope. As an almost universal rule we have never solved a problem on which our predecessors have worked in vain, unless through the discovery of some agency of which they had no conception. The demonstration that no possible combination of known substances, known forms of machinery, and known forms of force can be united in a practicable machine by which men shall fly long distances through the air, seems to the writer *as complete as it is possible for the demonstration of any physical fact to be.*

"But let us discover a substance a hundred times as strong as steel, and with that, some form of force hitherto unsuspected which will enable us to utilize this strength, *or* let us discover some way of reversing the law of gravitation, so that matter may be repelled by the earth instead of attracted — *then* we may have a flying machine. But we have every reason to believe that more ingenious contrivances with our present means and forms of force will be as vain in the future as they have been in the past."

In the light of the inductions of such eminent men, I wish again to impress the outlook for experimental work, for in the face of such adverse inductive opinions, Professor Samuel Langley and a few other minor workers excepted, Orville Wright demonstrated to the world that mechanical flight was wholly practicable with the materials we had and with the forms of energy already well known to us. It is my wish constantly to impress the reader that he does not have to have any particular cut and dried type of education for experimental success, and I wish to drive home that philosophy which lies at the foundation of all creative effort, that there are few real borderline limits, and practically no finality to sanely directed human effort. It was my pleasure and privilege to know Professor Langley here at Washington, and whereas I must confess that while the outlook for practical mechanical flight did not lead me to enthuse, it was always most painful to hear such serious efforts ridiculed.

Let me give another illustration of false borderline limits in an entirely different field, and the very fact that the problem was brilliantly solved should serve as a stimulus to other research workers in other fields.

More than thirty years ago Professor Charles E. Munroe began a study of the conditions of efficiency in the use of high explosives in attacks upon armor plate. At the Naval Ordnance Proving Ground, repeated charges of dynamite, varying from five pounds to one hundred pounds in weight, were detonated against the face of a vertical target consisting of eleven one-inch wrought-iron plates bolted to a twenty-inch oak backing, until four hundred and forty pounds of dynamite had been so detonated in contact with it, and yet the target remained practically uninjured. Professor Munroe wished to devise a high explosive and shell which would stand the shock of passing through the armor plate, and be detonated within the ship through the agency of a delayed action fuse. Shortly prior to 1898, due to his persistence and skill in this new art, he proved that a high explosive shell could stand such shock of impact and penetration, for a shell was fired through 14.5 inches of the Harveyized armor of the U.S.S. *Kentucky* and exploded on the inner side. So far as records go this achievement had never been approached. Like many other brilliant discoveries, our government failed to act as it might have in its recognition, and during the procrastination, I need not use a stronger word, it remained for the Japanese to demonstrate the armor piercing high explosive shell to the naval and military world. It has been my privilege to be an assistant of Professor Munroe's for many years past, and to his type of mind, which recognizes few barriers, the world owes the giant's share of its scientific progress.

But the foregoing engineering achievements were based upon a grasp of physical and chemical constants, and we may here have to recognize some borderline limits in such fundamentals, for example, as low and high temperatures. I cannot possibly illustrate this point any better than by quoting Professor Elihu Thomson, in his address before the American Association for the Advancement of Science, in which he said:

" Physical research by experimental methods is both a broadening and a narrowing field. There are many gaps yet to be filled, data to be accumulated, measurements to be made with great precision, but the limits within which we must work are becoming, at the same time, more and more defined. . . . The development in the field of research by experiment is like the opening of a mine, which, as it deepens and widens, continually yields new treasure, but with increased difficulty, except when a rich vein is struck and worked for a time. In general, however, as the work progresses there will be needed closer application and more refined methods. We may, indeed, find our limit of depth in the mine of experiment in inordinate cost, in temperatures too high, or in pressures beyond the limits of our skill to control. It is but a few months since Professor Dewar, by the evaporation of liquid hydrogen in a vacuum, closely approached, if he has not reached, our lower limit of possible temperature. Investigations of the effects of low temperature upon the properties of bodies must, from the present outlook, be forever limited to about 20 degrees Centigrade above absolute zero."

WILLIS RODNEY WHITNEY
Chemist, Research Director

Born at Jamestown, New York, August 22nd, 1868; S.B. Massachusetts Institute of Technology, 1890. Ph.D. University of Leipzig, 1896; Assistant Instructor, Assistant Professor, to 1904, non-resident Associate Professor, 1904 to 1918, non-resident Professor Theoretical Chemistry since 1908 Massachusetts Institute of Technology; Director Research Laboratory of General Electric Company, Schenectady, New York, since 1904.

Member of U. S. Naval Consulting Board since 1915; Member of National Research Council. Trustee Albany Medical College. Member National Academy of Sciences; Fellow American Academy of Arts and Sciences, A.A.A.S.; President American Chemical Society, 1910 (Willard Gibbs Medal, 1916).

American Electrochemical Society, 1911. Member Institute of Mining Engineers, American Institute of Electrical Engineers, etc.

Author: Translation of M. Le Blanc's "Electrochemistry," 1896, and contributor to many scientific magazines and to the transactions of professional societies.

Professor Thomson goes on to say that unless
a lighter gas than hydrogen be discovered upon
earth, the actual existence of which it is impossible to conjecture, the outlook for securing lower
temperatures is not promising. And this absolute zero is the temperature corresponding to a
total absence of heat. At the *absolute zero* the
molecules must be supposed to be *at rest*. At
this temperature gases (if they may be called
such) exert no pressure, and occupy no space
save that which their molecules take up when
closely packed together. The point of absolute
zero is independent of the conventions of man.
It is a point of absolute cold or total absence of
heat, beyond which no cooling is conceivable.
The pressure in air increases or diminishes by
.00367, which is equivalent to about $\frac{1}{273}$ of its
pressure at 0 degree for each centigrade degree
of rise or fall of temperature, the volume being
maintained constant. If the air were a perfect
gas, and could be cooled down to −273 degrees
Centigrade, it would cease to exert a pressure.
The reason it would exert no pressure is that
its particles would possess no kinetic energy,
no motion. This is assumed, therefore, to be
the absolute zero of temperature. We often
speak of temperature absolute, and degrees on
the absolute scale are found by adding 273 to
the readings on the Centigrade thermometer.
Thus 273 degrees absolute is 0 degrees Centi-

grade, 274 degrees absolute is 1 degree Centigrade, and 373 degrees absolute is 100 degrees Centigrade, or the boiling point of water. A number of years ago I was testing some apparatus to show that it would not burst or be otherwise disarranged by freezing, and my clients told me that they would not value my report unless I conducted the whole investigation at absolute zero! As I had a fee at stake, I could not diplomatically allow myself to crack a smile, and I set forth the above exposition of absolute zero with as long a drawn face as I could command!

But let me quote Professor Thomson's able address a little further where he takes us into the fairyland of high temperatures:

" While we may actually employ in electric furnaces temperatures which, according to Moissan, have a lower limit of 3500 degrees Centigrade, we can realize the possibility of temperatures existing in the stars measured by tens of thousands or hundreds of thousands of degrees of our temperature scale. The moderate increase of our working temperature given by the electric furnace enabled Moissan and others to reap a rich harvest of experimental results, and the natural inference is that much more might be expected from further extensions of the limits. These limits are, however, already set for us by the vaporization of all known substances. Our furnace itself keeps down the temperature by melting and volatilizing. We may indefinitely increase the energy in an electric arc and thus add to the heat evolved, but the addition only goes to vaporize more material."

This is analogous to adding fuel to the fire-box of a locomotive, without increasing the temperature of the water in the boiler; the energy goes into the latent heat of steam, propelling the engine without raising its temperature. " The limit of work," continued Professor Thomson,

"then seems to be readily reached in the electric furnace, no materials for lining being available, not subject either to fusion or vaporization, thus using up the energy which would otherwise go to increasing the temperature.

" A suggestion as to a possible extension of temperature range may be made here. It may be requisite to work with closed receptacles under pressure, and to discharge through them electric currents of so great energy value as to attain almost instantaneously the highest temperature, to be maintained for only a very short time.

" We may imagine a huge condenser charged to a potential of, say, 10,000 volts as discharged through a limited body of gas contained in a small space within a strong steel tube which has a lining of refractory non-conductor. The energy may thus possibly be delivered so suddenly to a very limited body of material as to result in a momentary elevation of temperature passing all present known limits and capable of effecting profound changes in molecular constitution."

It is often due to a simple little trick, although admittedly a very clever one, that a great new vein in experimental research is opened to the investigator, and the first suitably equipped worker with such a new tool may make his reputation and his fortune.

Then we have high vacua, and the inventions in high temperature filament lighting, in Röntgen rays, and the cathode streams and all the phenomena accompanying the passage of electricity through gases.

With all the varieties of piston and rotary pumps, the Geryk pump with its valves immersed in heavy oil, the mercury pump and the Gaede pump, known as the " Molecular " pump, for which it is claimed that a vacuum far beyond that of any other pump is attainable, there still remains room for advances.

The degree of efficiency reached by some of these pumps may be of interest here, and the following table sets forth approximately the relative value of vacuum pumps expressed in pressures in millimeters of mercury.

	Pressure in Mm. of Mercury
Water injector.	7.000
Sprengle (Mercury).	0.001
Geryk (Oil)	0.0002
Töpler (Mercury).	0.00001
Graede (Molecular).	0.0000002
Charcoal in Liquid Air.	0.0000008

Is this really the limit? Have we any sound reason for thinking that refinements or a totally different process of exhaustion should not give us much more perfect results?

On the other hand Professor Bridgeman has gone far into the region of high pressures of liquids and gases through the agency of his very simple but highly ingenious system of making gas-tight plugs and thread connections.

The present writer has been associated in the construction and use of high-pressure gas apparatus, which has held hydrogen securely under a pressure of 50,000 pounds to the square inch, by means of Bridgeman plugs and other fittings, and he has furthermore designed apparatus in which to conduct the electrolysis of solutions, insulating the electrodes successfully from the massive bomb container, and all under a pressure of 100,000 pounds to the square inch; and the only borderline limit that may be seen in this connection at the present time is the deformation pressure of special high-tensile-strength steels, which may be prepared for the purpose.

We thought we had reached the maximum range with our former artillery, and curiously enough mathematical and ballistic " experts " were demonstrating to me in the Ordnance Department the impossibility of the German seventy-five-mile gun, when I received advice from France that the weapon was an accomplished achievement. Who will venture an opinion as to the future limits of artillery fire, and who does not enjoy Jules Verne's graphic description of the great gun, which in his charming fiction fired a projectile from the earth to the moon? Who will venture an opinion on the future limits of high explosives, or on high voltages and high frequencies in alternating currents, or what fruits the extension of these fields may secure?

When electric sparks or a flaming electrical discharge is passed through air, some of the nitrogen is burned or oxidized to NO. How much? Alas, only about 2 per cent of the electrical energy supplied to the flame is useful in bringing about the permanent combination of nitrogen with oxygen. All the rest of the energy goes to waste, and try as we will to improve the efficiency of this very beautiful and simple method of " fixing " nitrogen, chemists and electricians have been unable to produce more than this miserable little yield. When we stop to realize that there are approximately 33,000 tons of free or uncombined nitrogen, but mechanically mixed with the oxygen of the air, of course, over every acre of ground and sea, it is exceedingly irritating to devise a combustion apparatus which fails to give us more than 2 per cent efficiency, when the NO formed reacts by itself in turn, without expenditure of additional power, with the oxygen of the air to form NO_2, and this in turn reacts automatically when brought into contact with water to form the indispensable HNO_3, which is nitric acid.

The limitation in the formation of NO — the first step in the process, is due to its breaking down again because its decomposition temperature lies within a few degrees of its formation temperature. It is this troublesome reverse reaction, or chemical equilibrium, which establishes itself, which prevents us from realizing an economic achievement. But let someone discover a chemical check valve, if I may use such an expression, to prevent this backslide, and the boon to agriculture and the arts and sciences in general would be enormous, and the inventor, if he knew how to protect himself, would make his everlasting fame and fortune. Do not be skeptical about the possibility of burning nitrogen in oxygen to a highly economic point, because it can be done, only just now we don't know how to do it.

Nitrogen is usually described as an inactive, inert, and lazy element, yet it has been known for a long time that vacuum tubes, containing nitrogen, frequently show a luminosity of this element after the discharge of electricity through the tube has taken place and has been cut off.

The glowing nitrogen has been shown to

have some very remarkable chemical properties. It combines quite readily now with
common phosphorous and at the same time
produces a great quantity of red phosphorous.
In its behavior, it resembles the halogens,
chlorine, bromine and iodine. The glowing
nitrogen also combines with sodium, with mercury and certain other metals, in each case
developing the line spectrum of the metal concerned.

In the molecule of high explosives we all
know its fierce activity. We have not begun
to reach the borderline limit of possibilities
with this remarkable sleepy element. Who will
wake it up? Who will secure the electric current direct from the oxidation of carbon, and
who will produce light without heat? There
are no borderline limits here; both things may
be accomplished, only just at present we miss
the little trick or the little key to enable us to
unlock the secret. The more we know in the
entire field of science, the better are we fitted
for attacking a specific problem. Science is
nothing more than a refined application of common sense, making the best possible use of
facts already known to acquire new facts.

Who believes for a minute that we have
reached the borderline limit in the storage
battery, that massive and cumbersome storage
tank discovered so long ago by Augustin Planté?

The storage cell today is fundamentally the same as it was when first discovered — two plates of lead suspended in water; and when a current of electricity is passed between them and through the water, hydrogen is thrown off at one plate, making it bright, and oxygen at the other plate, peroxidyzing its surface. When this current is discontinued and the altered plates are connected by means of a wire, the current is established in the opposite direction, and this continues until the plates reach their original condition. Hundreds of modifications have been made and patented, but no basic improvement has yet been realized, and he who succeeds in this field to extend the borderline of our knowledge here will indeed be rendering a superb service.

I might go on, of course, and cite case after case where we know perfectly well we are working within stupid and constricted areas, but anything like an attempt to make a complete list here would be outside of the domain of this little volume, and in this field of borderlines and human endeavor Sir William A. Tilden very beautifully expresses himself in the following lines:

"It is one of the characteristic features of modern physical science, which is not, like the ancient, content with observation of natural phenomena, but depends for progress on the results of experi-

not care to have experimental work and productive work under the same roof, and some refrain from spending a portion of their earnings upon research at all.

Dr. J. J. Carty, or to attempt to keep up to date some of these military titles, Colonel Carty, compares research pure and applied in the factory in the following picturesque manner:

"The investigator in pure science may be likened to the explorer who discovers new continents or islands or hitherto unknown territory. He is continually seeking to extend the boundaries of knowledge. The investigator in industrial research may be compared to the pioneers who survey the newly discovered territory in the endeavor to locate its mineral resources, determine the extent of its forests, and the location of its arable land, and who in other ways precede the settlers and prepare for their occupation of the new territory."

Now let us prepare, and lose no more time in occupying this new territory, for new territory it is in America, for skillful and highly organized workers.

I have in a previous chapter made the statement that America, in contrast with the old world, could not honestly claim to be a nation of commercial and especially chemical research, and I attempted to drive home the fact that research in our factories was not at the highest activity.

Dr. G. W. Thomson, President of the American Institute of Chemical Engineers, said very recently:

" We learn by adversity. This war has taught us that all industry is more or less chemical in its character. . . . Practical business men often distrust college professors. They say they are all theoretical and visionary. This is in many cases due to the fact that the practical business man has a narrow vision. Sometimes it may be true that instructors in chemistry have not a practical turn of mind. . . . It is my opinion that the educational institutions of the country should give honorary degrees to men who have accomplished big things in the industrial world.

" The practice in many of these institutions is to give degrees only to those who have done original work in what is called pure science. . . . Manufacturers can do a great deal to help the universities and colleges in developing more efficient methods of instruction. . . . That while it is extremely interesting and upbuilding to think in terms of atoms and molecules, it is equally important to think in terms of large quantities of the chemical compounds that enter into reactions."

The point which Dr. Thomson brings out, that the manufacturer can be very helpful to the college man, is most important, as well as his suggestion that the theorist should become a bit more practical by thinking in the larger nomenclature of factory terms.

The beautiful generalization which Colonel Carty has given us for research in the factory may be visualized in connection with the wisdom expressed by Dr. Thomson in a specific case, and we may perhaps choose to advantage the laboratory discovery dealing in atoms and molecules, of nitrocellulose, and the subsequent manufacture of smokeless powder dealing in tons, an art with which I am more or less familiar from experience in explosive laboratory and factory.

The basic scientific principle was discovered in the laboratory upon a minute scale through the treating of cellulose with concentrated nitric and sulphuric acids, with the subsequent researches in its collodizing and graining. Then researches had to be made proving that it could be used to burn progressively, instead of detonating in the gun. From this point on we may regard the product as a laboratory-proving-ground-factory product. It would be manifestly impractical and unsafe to separate one of these essential arts from the other. It is only through the briskest coöperation of the professor, the experimentalist, and the practical manufacturer that such a substance as smokeless powder could have been discovered and developed — or to express it technically, " reduced to practice."

The discovery that cellulose may be converted

into a highly explosive body, by treatment with strong nitric acid, was made in the laboratory during the first half of the nineteenth century. Braconnot made important experiments with nitric acid and organic matter in 1833, and Pelouze prepared explosive bodies in 1838, from nitric acid, a paper, linen, and starch and Schonbein discovered that cellulose in the form of cotton, when treated with nitric acid, and properly washed and dried afterward, gave a highly explosive compound. This substance became known as guncotton and today forms the basis of all modern smokeless powders. When this substance was first studied, it was welcomed by military experts as a wonderful substitute for the old-fashioned gunpowder which burned with such dense clouds of smoke. It took the combined talents of chemical professors in the laboratory, and of technologists in the factory, and of artillery specialists on the proving ground to secure and control its rate of combustion. Many unlooked-for detonations took place in pieces of artillery of various calibers with many disastrous results in the progress of experiments, and finally it was found to be so very dangerous that its use was abandoned. Over forty years elapsed before this combination of college professor, powdermaker and artillery expert learned how to prepare and control this explosive cellulose in guns.

Among the most brilliant workers in this field was Dr. Charles Edward Munroe, who made great advances in its graining, freeing it from tendencies from detonation in the gun, from producing undue erosion, and in giving the powder keeping qualities and maximum propulsion value. I know of no other art, wherein the theories in the laboratory, the practical manufacturer, and the research experimenter were required to carry out closer harmony of work than in this dangerous type of problem.

We speak of the skill and accuracy of our naval and military gunners, and we are thoughtlessly inclined to give them and the gun-makers credit for *all* the skill when repeated hits are made.

The gunners are highly trained men and their great guns are well designed and constructed, but we should not forget the research worker and the manufacturer of the propellent, for if the research worker here in the laboratory-factory had not standardized his cellulose, and had not treated it according to standard methods with standard acids, or employed standardized methods of collodizing and standard manipulaions in a score or more other points, do you suppose for an instant that upon the recoil of the great piece of artillery in which a definite weight of powder is fired, that the projectile in its flight would describe the same trajectory as

it did a minute, an hour, a week or a month before when the gun was set to the same elevation? How could the physician prescribe with
any degree of safety or confidence nitrogly-
cerine for heart action, or any other chemical
prescription unless he knew the many qualities
of his ingredients were properly standardized
and kept so in the factory?

It may be of interest here to analyze a little
more in detail a factory or two with which I
have first-hand knowledge, and see how a chemist or a physicist or an engineer is helpful and
often absolutely necessary to the manufacturer
turning out a product which apparently has no
points of contact with either of these basic
sciences.

I will take up for the purpose of illustration
the case of an adding machine with which I
had to do in its factory development. The
theory and computations of the design had
been completed, and very cleverly completed,
by an apt and able inventor in this line of endeavor, and it remained only to redesign its
details and specify the materials of its various
parts in order that the machine could be economically constructed, and so it could compete
profitably with the other machines already on
the market. The machine had to be of the
lightest weight consistent with strength and
stiffness of its frame and movable parts, which

necessitated, of course, that every piece which
entered into its construction had to be made of
the most suitable metal or alloy or of the precise character of steel of the very best composition. Its keys and levers, as well as the glass
paneled housing, had also to be fool-proof, bug-
proof and rust-proof. The enamel work, the
nickel plating, the case-hardening of the wearing
parts, the composition and tempering, and resili-
ency of its springs, the application of lock-nuts
where anything could shake loose in use or transportation, all require critical study before making
the dies and jigs for turning out the parts, for
it was necessary, of course, that the machine
operate perfectly after its first assembly, and
that it be capable of standing rough and careless use, and that after tens of thousands of
manipulations of its keys and levers, it would
not be weak in any spot. Like almost any perfectly designed machine, it should theoretically
be like the old doctor's " one-horse shay," which,
when it had served its long and honorable
career, dropped completely apart! This involved
a study of all exceptionally active members,
properly hardening them wherever wear comes
into play, and with all, it must be seen that the
design permits interchangeable parts for large
quantity, economical production. It is, of course,
impossible, no matter how close the scientific
control or how minute the mechanical study

may be projected, in planning for the construction of such a machine in quantities, that the ultimate be attained in the first cast. There is always a chance even in the fifth and sixth and seventh editions for minor, and sometimes major improvements, which it appears in the present state of our constructive knowledge cannot be fully anticipated. Typographical errors persist in eluding galley and page proofreaders, and frequently stare at one from the pages of a book that has received the ablest criticism, not only in the composition room, but by outside proofreaders and the author.

It will, therefore, be apparent that the more systematic the research work, and the more painstaking the study in the factory, the greater the ultimate saving in cost of labor and material, and the quicker the crystallization of the ultimate perfect machine. Few instances where haste makes waste are more substantiated in practice than in the lack of systematic research work in connection with the factory product.

In the case of the development of a high tension electrical magneto, as another example, the specifications of the magnet-steel were of vital importance. The magnetization of the steel, the ageing and final testing, the character and thickness of the lamination punching, for the rotor, the composition of the enamel wire of the windings, the insulating compounds and waterproof varnishes, for sustained operation in all climates, had to be minutely studied in connection with the theory and practice of the roughest kind of operation. Unless all the phases of construction of such a machine, designed for a certain purpose, are fully anticipated and carefully worked out, a factory will find that it is junking model after model, with all the frightfully expensive labor, tools and jigs, as a new and more perfect machine develops itself. Very few people realize what a tremendous loss of labor and material takes place for lack of proper design and research education by those entrusted with the work of producing an ultimate factory product.

These are easy and simple mechanical and electrical cases, however, because I have purposely chosen types of factory products that are comparatively simple and where *full-scale* experiments are in reality, *small-scale* experiments, and are most conveniently handled in the experimental shop of the factory. But there are the troublesome cases also where experiments have to be made upon a very great scale, as in our smokeless powder development, before the design of a device may be successfully completed, and here the question of mistakes or unforeseen mistaken policies work greater havoc still, with material and labor. Consider an electric locomotive or a steam turbine, in its development, or consider for a moment the character of experimental work and the experimental scale necessary in the economical perfection of the design of a switch for opening and closing a high-tension electrical power circuit, or in designing the porcelain insulators and lightning arresters for installation in such work. Only at certain laboratories or in connection with experimental transmission lines on a large and full sized scale, can data of real and practical worth be obtained. The design of all high voltage transmission lines and accessory apparatus was, of course, based upon laboratory full-scale experiments on the electric strength of air under all conditions of moisture and temperature, and on the losses in the electrostatic corona around insulators and line. Dr. Charles P. Steinmetz said in connection with this class of full-scale work:

" Unfortunately, this limitation of research work in accordance with the available facilities is not always realized, and especially educational institutions not infrequently attempt research work, for which industrial laboratories are far better fitted, while research work for which the educational institution is well fitted, which the industry needs but cannot economically undertake, is left undone."

A scheme of industrial research to meet such difficult cases was proposed a short time ago by the late Professor Kennedy Duncan involving the use of industrial fellowships at universities. This plan was proposed to be one of value to manufacturers who did not care, for one reason or another, to equip and maintain their own laboratories. It has been said that American manufacturers have, unlike the Germans, been accustomed to steer clear of theorists and especially of chemists. Ellwood Hendrick writes:

" The main feature, however, is that German business men are not afraid of that bugaboo of his American cousin, to-wit, 'the theorist.' American capitalists will take up an engineering problem and look over blue-prints and plotted curves which they do not completely understand, but which they will try to grasp, and as soon as they get the idea of what is to be accomplished and a theory of the method, down comes the telephone receiver, and a syndicate is formed. The money is straightway available. If the problem is a chemical one, it has been his habit to close his mind and his eye and to have nothing to do with it, whereas his counterpart in Germany would go at the proposal with the same lively curiosity and interest that he would display in response to a proposal in engineering. The result is that the American business man has neither experience in, nor knowledge of, chemistry. He cannot tell one chemist from another. He doesn't even know where to go to find out. Not long ago some Eastern capitalists took under consideration a large investment in a chemical works engaged in the utmost niceties of chemical manufacture. The processes were involved and exceedingly complex. So, in order to get at the bottom facts concerning the industry and the way the problems were met, they sent a civil engineer out to examine it. They might as well have sent a dentist! "

A manufacturer in need of specialized knowledge and expert laboratory experimentation would, under Professor Kennedy Duncan's scheme, write to one of the universities providing industrial fellowships. The man deemed best fitted for the special work in hand is chosen by the chancellor of the university and the industrial fellowship is installed with a special research laboratory, often designed and constructed for large scale experiments, with materials and supplies from the interested manufacturer.

This manufacturer provides the working funds and the compensation for the fellow. In the working out of the scheme any discoveries or inventions in the art which may be made by the research fellow become the property of the manufacturer, subject to the payment of a royalty or other interest in the property, the amount of which is determined by a Board of Arbitration provided for in the plan.

There were, of course, many additional details of equal interest involved in the working out of the scheme and provided for in Professor Duncan's report. The scheme was actually in use for four years, during which time eighteen fellowships have been established in the University of Kansas and twenty were planned for in the University of Pittsburg. Some manufacturers, on the other hand, are not so mortally afraid of theories, and equip their factories with the most up-to-date research laboratories of their own on their premises, and employ the ablest specialists they can secure. This method, is, of course, the most expensive. I will not say the most costly, for it has been truly said that "Unless industrial research abundantly supports itself, it will have failed of its purpose."

And this question of invention and compensation therefore, — since there are sure to come up, if a young research worker is engaged in the experimental department of a manufacturing company, some of the phases of his relationship with the company if he makes an invention while in the employ of the corporation,—may be of interest and value here.

In connection with the employer and employee it may be made as a general statement that no statutory provision exists except that relating to Government employees. Those provisions and the special rulings as to employees of the Government may be learned under the title *Government* in "The Fixed Law of Patents," second edition, by William Macomber. Questions of title and rights as between employers and employees will also be found under *assignment* and *licenses* in this comprehensive book.

But we are primarily interested in research in the factory here, and we will leave the Government references for those who may have occasion to look them up, and quote from a number of actual court cases and court rulings in instances of research worker and the employer in commercial enterprises.

Of course no references of this character can be strictly up to date, but the following will serve to show the character of court rulings in the past and I see no reasons for radical departures from the character of these decisions.

"Article 365. *Contract—Future Inventions.—* Complainant and defendant contracted that in consideration of the employment of defendant and wages paid him, defendant would give complainant the exclusive use of any improvements he might make upon their particular machines while in their employ or after. *Held:* Such argument to be neither unconscionable, unreasonable nor contrary to public policy. Bonsack *v.* Hulse, 65 Fed. 864; 13 C. C. A. 180.

"Registering Co. *v.* Sampson, L. R. 19 Eq. 465, 1 Sedg. Dam. 455; Horner *v.* Graves, 7 Bing.

735; Ammuition *v.* Nordenfelt, 1 Ch. 630; Match *v.* Rosler, 106 N. Y. 473; Morse *v.* Morse, 103 Mass. 73.

" We now pass to the defense that the contract was not enforceable in equity upon the theory of lack of consideration and lack of mutuality. This contract, however, was not without consideration. It was not only by its own express terms in consideration of the employment of the defendant, but this contract was signed and delivered before the employment actually commenced, and before the defendant was permitted to enter the complainant's factory. The hiring, the engagement to pay wages and the introduction of the defendant into the complainant's establishment and to its methods and processes, constituted a valid consideration for his agreement to assign his inventions made during the term of employment. — Mississippi *v.* Franzen, 143 Fed. 501; 74 C. C. A. 135.

" Bonsack *v.* Hulse, 65 Fed. 864; Thibodeau *v.* Hildreth, 124 Fed. 892; Rob. Pat. Sec. 414; Green *v.* Richards, 23 N. J. Eq. 32, 35; Grove *v.* Hodge, 55 Pa. 501, 516.

" Where the employee invents in the line of his employment with the tools and at the expense of his employer, the fact that his wages are not increased on account of such services as was in the case in McClurg *v.* Kingsland, 42 U. S. 202, makes no vital difference. — Solomons *v.* U. S. 137 U. S. 342; 34 L. Ed. 667; 11 S. Ct. 88.

" When the employee allows his invention to be

constructed and used by his employer before patent he cannot claim royalty or right of injunction thereafter. Dable *v*. Flint, 137 U. S. 41; 34 L. Ed. 618; 11 S. Ct. 8; Wade *v*. Metcalf, 129 U. S. 202.

" Where employee makes an invention in the shops and with the tools of the employer, the employer gains an implied license, and such implied license may be succeeded to by a corporation as successor in business, if such course is acquiesced in by the inventor. — Lane *v*. Locke, 150 U. S. 193; 37 L. Ed. 1049; 14 S. Ct. 78.

" McClurg *v*. Kingsland, 42 U. S. 202; Solomon *v*. U. S. 137 U. S. 342.

" When an employee made and introduced his invention in employer's furnaces and told his employer he could use the same so long as he remained in defendant's employ, such facts gave defendant an implied license, at least during the period of employment of plaintiff. — Keyes *v*. Eureka, 158 U. S. 150; 39 L. Ed. 920; 15 S. Ct. 772.

" The fact that the invention was made and the drawings prepared outside the hours and the shops of the employer, so long as the invention was reduced to practice and made in the employer's shops by the employee and with his consent, does not secure him the right to damages for infringement by his employer. — Gill *v*. U. S. 160 U. S. 426; 40 L. Ed. 480; 16 S. Ct. 322.

" An employee paid by salary or wages who devises an important method of doing his work, using the property or labor of his employer to put his invention into practical form, and assenting to the use of such improvements by his employer, cannot, by taking out a patent upon such invention, recover a royalty or other compensation for such use. — Gill *v*. U. S. 160 U. S. 426; 40 L. Ed. 480; 16 S. Ct. 322.

" Pennock *v*. Dialogue, 23 U. S. 1; Grant *v*. Raymond, 31 U. S. 218; McClurg *v*. Kingsland, 42 U. S. 202; Solomons *v*. U. S. 137 U. S. 342; Lane *v*. Locke, 150 U. S. 193; McAleer *v*. U. S. 150 U. S. 424; Keyes *v*. Eureka, 158 U. S. 150.

" There was some evidence to show that the original patterns were destroyed by fire before the machines sold by appellant were made, and it is insisted that the scope of the license should be limited by the life of the identical patterns. The duration and scope of a license must depend upon the nature of the invention and the circumstances out of which an implied license is presumed, and both must at last depend upon the intention of the parties. — Witherington *v*. Kinney, 68 Fed. 500; 15 C. C. A. 531.

"Rob. Pat. Secs. 809–811; Montross *v*. Mabie, 30 Fed. 4.

" Complainant was employed as an expert machinist to devise and construct an improved machine and to direct the making of patterns for the same for machine to be made and sold. Later, complainant obtained a patent, and after ten years brought suit. *Held:* Upon this store of facts we conclude that the appellee must be presumed to

have granted to appellant's licensor a personal
license to make and sell machines embodying the
improvements covered by his patent. — Witherington *v.* Kinney, 68 Fed. 500; 15 C. C. A. 531.

"McClurg *v.* Kingsland, 1 How. 202; Solomons
v. U. S. 137 U. S. 342; Lane *v.* Locke, 150 U. S.
193; Hapgood *v.* Hewitt, 119 U. S. 226.

" The cases, therefore, of an inventor who was
a workman in the employ of another, manufactures
for him, in his shop, and with his materials, and
upon weekly wages, machines which the employer
uses as part of his tools without knowledge of any
objection thereto, and for which the inventor during the terms of his employment obtains a patent
and thereafter seeks to restrain the employer from
the use of the particular machine or machines
which had been thus made in the employer's shop,
under the supervision of the employee, and apparently as a part of his ordinary mechanical work.
On the authority of Gill *v.* U. S. 160 U. S. 426, the
employee-patentee was estopped. — Blauvelt *v.*
Interior, 80 Fed. 906; 26 C. C. A. 243.

" Paragraph 367. *Rights of Employee.* Persons
employed, as much as employers, are entitled to
their own independent inventions, and if the suggestions communicated constitute the whole substance of the improvement the rule is otherwise,
and the patent, if granted to the employer, is invalid, because the real invention or discovery be-
longs to the person who made the suggestion. —
Union *v.* Vandeusen, 90 U. S. 530; 23 L. Ed. 128;
Agawam *v.* Jordan, 7 Wall 602.

"When a person has discovered a new and useful principle in a machine, manufacture or composition of matter, he may employ other persons to assist in carrying out that principle, and if they, in the course of experiments arising from that employment, make discoveries ancillary to the planned and preconceived design of the employer, such suggested improvements are in general to be regarded as the property of the party who discovered the original principle, and they may be embodied in his patent as part of his invention. — Union v. Vandeusen, 90 U. S. 530; 23 L. Ed. 128.

" As to rights of a person employed to invent, see Hapgood v. Hewett, 118; U. S. 226; 30 L. Ed. 369; 7 S. Ct. 193; McClurg v. Kingsland, 42 U. S. 202; Continental v. Empire, 8 Blatchf. 295; Whiting v. Graves, 3 B. & A. 222, Wilkins v. Spafford, 3 B. & A. 274.

" In the absence of evidence of an agreement that the employer should have any interests in any patentable improvement which the employee might make during the period of his employment, it would seem that the title to the invention made or to any patent subsequently obtained by him, would be unaffected by the fact of his service, and in the use of his employer's shop, materials and the service of his employees while devising and perfecting his invention. — Withington v. Kinney, 68 Fed. 500; 15 C. C. A. 531; Hapgood v. Hewett, 119 U. S. 226.

" Article 368.   *Rights of Employer.* — The inventor, while in the employ of the defendant, made his invention and perfected the same with the

tools and while under pay of the defendant, and
in his shop. Defendant increased the inventor's
wages by reason of such invention. The invention
was put in practice by plaintiff in defendant's
shops and used without any agreement or license.
Subsequently the inventor quit from another cause
and suit was brought. *Held:* That such employment and conduct gave the employer a shop right
to said invention. McClurg *v.* Kingsland, 1 How.
202; 11 L. Ed. 102.

"*Note:* This leading case has generally been
construed too broadly. The court did not hold in
expressed terms that the mere employment or the
extra pay constituted the license, independent of
the subsequent conduct. This case is good for
what it holds, but it by no means establishes the
relation of employer and employee definitely.

" Persons employed, as much as employers, are
entitled to their own independent inventions, but
where the employer has conceived the plan of an
invention and is engaged in experiments to perfect
it, no suggestion from an employee, not amounting to a new method or arrangement, is sufficient
to deprive the employer of the exclusive property
in the perfected improvement. But where the
suggestions go to make up a complete and perfect
machine, embracing the substance of all that is
embodied in the patent subsequently issued to the
party to whom the suggestions were made, the
patent is invalid, because the real invention or discovery belonged to another.—Agawam *v.* Jordan,
74 U. S. 583; 19 L. Ed. 177.

" Pits *v.* Hall, 2 Blatchf. 234; Allen *v.* Rawson,
1 Man. G. & F. 574; Alden *v.* Dewey, 1 Storey,
336; Minters Pat. 1 Web. P. C. 132; Curt. Pat.
99; Reed *v.* Cutter, 1 Story, 599.

" No one is entitled to a patent for that which
he did not invent unless he can show a legal title
to the same from the inventor or by operation of
law; but when a person has discovered an improved principle in a machine, manufacture or
composition of matter, and employs other persons
to assist him in carrying out the principle, and they
in the course of experiments arising from that employment make valuable discoveries ancillary to
the plan and preconceived design of the employer,
such suggested improvements are in general to
be regarded as the property of the party who discovered the original improved principle, and may
be embodied in his patent as a part of his invention.
— Agawam *v.* Jordan, 74 U.S. 583; 19 L. Ed. 177.

" A manufacturing corporation which has employed a skilled workman, for stated compensation,
to take charge of its works, and to devote his time
and services to devising and making improvements
in articles there manufactured, is not entitled to a
conveyance of patents obtained for inventions made
by him while so employed, in the absence of express agreement to that effect. — Dalzell *v.* Deuber,
149 U. S. 315; 37 L. Ed. 749, 13 S. Ct. 886; Hapgood *v.* Hewett, 119 U. S. 226.

" That an agreement by an employee to keep
forever secret for the benefit of employer any invention or discovery he may make during the term

of his employment, is not unconscionable, see
Thibodeau *v.* Hildreth, 124 Fed. 892; 60 C. C. A.
78.

" We do not think that the defendant is estopped
by reason of the relation of the parties and his
own conduct, to deny such equitable title in complainant. Both must rest upon the same basis of
fact and law. Whether the complainant would
have been justified in claiming what is called a
shop right or a right to a license, irrevocable or
otherwise, is not the question raised by its bill.
The claim is for the whole an exclusive title, and
the demand for a legal assignment of the same.
— Pressed Steel *v.* Hansen, 137 Fed. 403; 71
C. C. A. 207.

"Article 369. — *Miscellaneous Rulings.* Suggestions from another, made during the progress of
experiments, in order that they may be sufficient
to defeat a patent subsequently issued, must have
embraced the plan of improvement and must have
furnished such information to whom the communication was made that it would have enabled an
ordinary mechanic, without the exercise of any
ingenuity and special skill on his part, to construct
and put the improvement in successfull operation.
— Agawam *v.* Jordan, 74 U. S. 583; 19 L. Ed. 177.

" This evidence brings the case clearly within
the terms of the decision of McClurg *v.* Kingsland,
1 How. 202, where it was declared that if a person
employed in the manufactory of another, while re-
ceiving wages, makes experiments at the expense
and in the manufactory of the employer, has his

wages increased in consequence of the useful
result of experiment, makes the article invented,
and permits his employer to use it, no compensation for its use being paid or demanded, and then
obtains a patent for it, the patent is invalid and
void.

" And as the employer could defend himself on
the ground of public use, so could a third person.

" And the fact that the employer just before
application purchased an interest in the patent to
be granted does not avoid the fact of public use
by him. — Worley *v.* Loker, 104 U. S. 340; 26
L. Ed. 821.

" Pardy was a mechanic and patent solicitor.
Hooker employed him to get up a machine and
gave Pardy his own ideas as to how the desired
result could be accomplished. The agreement was
that Hooker was to pay all cost of the work and pay
Pardy for his services, and was to own and control
the patent that should be issued covering the machine. Hooker paid all the cost of the machines
and paid Pardy in full. We are of opinion that such
suit (for infringement) cannot be sustained, in
view of the distinct agreement between Hooker
and Pardy. We are of the opinion, however, that
the court below was, in view of the evidence, in
error in adjudging Pardy was not the inventor of
the machine patented. Hooker knew, or must be
held to have known, that such patent could not
have been issued except upon the oath that Pardy
was the inventor. Hooker did not himself apply
for such patent, and there is nothing to indicate

that he ever contemplated doing so. It is true, as has been said, that he gave Pardy his own ideas and employed him to get up such a machine as he (Hooker) desired. But the accomplishment of the desired end was evidently left to Pardy. The court should not have adjudged the patent to be void, or that Pardy was not the inventor. — Pardy v. Hooker, 148 Fed. 631; 78 C. C. A. 403."

I am indebted to all of these foregoing concise rulings with references to "The Fixed Law of Patents," second edition, by William Macomber, Lecturer on Law of Patents in Cornell University College of Law.

One of the practices for stimulating inquiry in the research laboratories of a great and progressive American industry today is to have definite agreements and understandings with the research workers as to inventions and daily conferences of the research workers in the various laboratories and construction departments of the plant. Each week certain problems form the basis of a more general and formal meeting, with all of the laboratory workers together, the technical men in other than laboratory phases, and with the chairman present, acting as the director of the conference. Thus a happy and amicable research family may be established and run and the problems viewed and attacked from many angles.

CHAPTER VIII

The Making and Protecting of Inventions

THE usefulness and often brilliance of inventions springing from Yankee mental activity cannot be denied, and should not be discounted, yet on the other hand, as has been pointed out by others in the preface, and in previous chapters of this little book, thousands of misguided inventors apply for patents every month, and spend their hundreds, and often thousands of dollars, and months, and often years, upon old or worthless conceptions.

I hope very sincerely that I may in the following pages, through telling what I know from long experience in this field, add at least a tiny mite toward preventing future disappointments, and in raising inventive efficiency, if I may use such a term.

There are tens of thousands of actual patents taken out annually that are absolutely of no value, either because the history of the activity in this line, " the prior art," as it is technically called, makes them void, or because they are necessarily narrow in the language of their claims, covering only unimportant detail portions of an old and previously patented device.

There are many with genuine talent for inventing, but with an absolute lack of knowledge of a patent, of the merits or demerits of its specification and claims, and there are unfortunately scores of unscrupulous patent attorneys and patent firms who advertise elaborately to ensnare this class of ignorant inventor, and who thrive off the gullibility of their clients.

If you have an idea which you believe to be good, the sooner you know if it is really valuable or not, the better. Don't, therefore, be too secretive, or suspicious of those who may really help you, by letting you know if the idea is new and sound and valuable, and rush off to an advertising patent attorney for " a free opinion as to patentability," for there is an immense gulf between the novelty, soundness, and value of an idea, and its patentability, and there is almost a certainty that the patent attorney will set his cap for your money and write back, "We are of the opinion that your invention can be patented."

Possibly it can, I freely grant this, but the patent would in all probability not be of the slightest real value when issued, owing to the scores or hundreds in the same line that have been patented before.

Does this class of attorney really know this state of affairs when he encourages you to take out another patent? Of course he does! How am I so certain? Because, having a natural passion for research and investigation in human matters, as well as in matters technological, I have either visited personally, or written or sent an investigator to secure data for me, to many of these attorneys and firms with carefully selected "chestnut" ideas on record in the patent office files and as old as Methuselah, and without exception it was suggested or urged that a patent be applied for.

The United States Commissioner of Patents has frequently had his attention directed to this evil, and I think we may soon look for modifications of the flamboyant advertisements of this class of attorney and patent firm we see in so many of our popular scientific and engineering magazines.

As I told the present Commissioner not long since, the public would be surprised and shocked to know of the magnitude of the traffic encouraged by patent law sharks. There exists today as great a need for a campaign against such parasites as there was against fraudulent patent medicines and "phony" gold mining stocks, and I think we may look for some marked improvement under the incumbency of the present Commissioner.

An examination of the myriads of duplication work in many classes in United States cases in the American Patent Office shows up clearly also this unhappy accumulated traffic. And as for foreign applications made in our patent office, this wasteful duplication is far less marked.

By order of the Secretary of War and the Chief of Ordnance, I was instructed to examine the patent applications that pertained to military matters in the secret archives of the Patent Office, and especially the cases of alien enemies, in quest of useful knowledge for our Government, and to report to a committee which United States patents should be withheld from issuance to prevent useful knowledge reaching the enemy. The contrast between duplication work by inventors here and abroad was very marked, in favor of foreign economic endeavors.

It is one thing to invent an ingenious but commercially impractical thing, and quite another art to invent an equally or even less ingenious, but cleverly practical device also. The great Bessemer art of making steel from molten iron, by blowing air through it to burn away the excess carbon, was not nearly so ingenious and meritorious from the point of view of mental equipment and exercise, as it worked out to be practical. It worked, and moreover the heat of combustion of the carbon in the molten iron with the oxygen of the air blown into the converter was sufficient to keep the iron molten until it was converted into steel. It was a beautifully practical process, but one requiring no very profound knowledge.

Broadly speaking, inventors are found divided into two great classes. — First, the inventors of simple novelties, toys, and small time and labor saving devices. Such inventions, when new and ingenious and commercially easy of manufacture and practical, are almost always, when skillfully patented and well managed, good money makers.

This class of invention requires but little technical education, if any, and no engineering talent, except the talent for what may be called human engineering. This human engineering consists largely in getting the proper associate or associates to assist in the financing and marketing of the perfected invention. In general it is safest to steer clear of inventions along popular lines for the reason that the archives of the patent office are crowded more than ever with these classes, and in the field where so many patents are issued daily, each patent more or less conflicts with the other, and a manufacturer undertaking to develop and put upon the market any one of such so-called inventions, lays himself open to patent suits from other and disgruntled inventors in the same line. So it must be appreciated that every invention in any one class depends for its validity upon preceding ones, and conflicting claims are frequent among inventors who do not appreciate the status or bearing of the prior art.

Before applying for a patent for a novelty in this class of invention, it would be wise in addition to securing the information already recommended to have some one make a really good search of the archives and send copies of all the patents issued in this art; they may be had for five cents apiece, or better still, in the interest of education in inventive engineering, if I may coin such an expression, if the inventor can afford it, let him come to Washington and study the patent office system a bit by looking through the files himself. They are open to anyone, attorney, student and inventor alike, who wishes to make a search. Or if this is not feasible, let the inventor find a reliable representative at Washington to make the search and report to him.

The other great class of inventors, which this book is primarily intended to assist, includes technology in the engineering sense, but successful inventions in this line are usually only the outcome of many months and often years of study and experiment.

As a rule the most successful inventors are those who have been competently advised to take up some special line of endeavor, and then devote their best energies to its development.

It is especially sad and unfortunate for a man to work for years along barren lines, when a little contact with engineers in advance would have saved him all the work and disappointment.

But success in major or technological inventions requires more than ever a reliable insight of what is really needed, coupled with a pretty thorough knowledge of the prior art.

"When planning some research or invention," writes Professor V. Karapetoff, a well-known electrical engineer, "try to think of it in the light of the past and future development of the subject, not as a detached little investigation of your own. . . . There are problems on which no one is working, either because the situation is premature or because others became discouraged through lack of results."

This is first class advice and should be carefully heeded. If you have an idea, therefore, examine it from all angles, preferably in the following order.

Is the principle technically sound?

Can it be economically manufactured and marketed?

Is there really room for it or an active demand?

What is the status of the prior art?

Can I secure a purchaser, or a manufacturer?

If you are unable to answer these questions yourself, exercise a little of the human engineering and get in touch with some one who can. But you may feel in your bones, even if you will not admit it, that you are distrustful and fear your idea may be stolen. Very good — then protect yourself in a preliminary way by writing a full and comprehensive description of the invention, making sketches or drawings integral with the description, all in ink, dated and signed, and the signature witnessed by several well known citizens of repute in your town. Several copies, all in ink, similarly signed and witnessed, should be made and several may be turned over to some one outside of your office or shop for safe keeping.

When this is done you are fairly safe and this signed and witnessed instrument may be accepted as evidence of conception with the date thereon in case of conflict with others.

The average inventor, and I know the species well, is apt to be too secretive, and he loses much of his efficiency through this fault, if fault it can always be called. There are at least a hundred men who would help you to one crooked fellow who would steal your idea, and the plans of this thief may be frustrated by the signed instrument I have just suggested.

A research worker, who may decide to make invention a business, should develop this human element in engineering by acquiring a knowledge of just who to go to for preliminary advice, as well as for possible assistance later in the matter of exploitation — an art in itself.

The inventor should cultivate this working knowledge of men just as he may have acquired a working knowledge of scientific and engineering catalogues, and with the files of the technical periodicals in his own line and with the pertinent best books in a great library. Sometimes a reference to a book unknown to a research worker will be worth more than one can estimate. I have had references furnished to me by specialist friends that have saved me weeks and months of hard work.

And speaking of magazines and books, and the value of references, a very high percentage of American inventors, especially those of the less educated or mechanic class, understand or appreciate neither of two great fundamental facts in the patent law of this country, and these have to do with the vital bearing of " Prior use " or " Prior publication " upon the value of an invention or the validity of a patent. Let me quote a few lines from the Statutory Provisions of the United States Patent Office relative to the securing of a valid patent:

" Any person who has invented or discovered any new and useful art, machine, manufacture, or composition of matter, or any new and useful improvements thereof, not known or used by thers in this country, *before his invention thereof,* and not patented or described in any printed publication in this or any foreign country, before his invention or discovery thereof, *or more than two years prior to his application,* and not in public use or on sale in this country for more than two years prior to his application, unless the same is proved to have been abandoned, may, upon payment of the fees required by law, and other due proceedings had, obtain a patent therefor."

On the filing of any such application and the payment of the fees required by law, the Commissioner of Patents shall cause an examination to be made of the alleged new invention or discovery; and if on such examination it shall appear that the claimant is justly entitled to a patent under the law and that the same is sufficiently useful and important, the Commissioner shall issue a patent therefor.

The terms " new and useful " govern in a broad way the validity of an invention. Any existing foreign patents or description of the invention contained in any regular publication in any part of the world, prior to making an invention, renders a patent null and void. If a United States Patent has been issued by a careless examiner, and there are unfortunately such in our patent office, and signed, sealed and delivered by the United States Patent Office, with its red seal and blue ribbon, it is not generally appreciated that the patent is worthless, if one can point to a published description of the device in any periodical in any language before the invention was made. Clearly, if such a published account existed, the invention was not "*new*" according to the terms of the statutory provision already quoted.

I remember being retained as an " expert " in a patent suit over which many thousands of dollars were being spent. A bomb-shell was virtually exploded in the court room when I was enabled to point out from my studies that an Italian scientific magazine had described the device quite fully six years before the United States Patent Office issued the patent! Both sides in the case were a sorry looking lot, and if I had not made the discovery someone else probably would have done so later. In the case of a perfectly valid patent, where no previous description can be discovered, it is not generally appreciated that the protection of the device lies wholly in the language of the " claims " as allowed. These claims may be broad and basic, and on the other hand they may be involved and narrow. The showy drawings, or the full description of the invention in the specifications, do not afford the protection, but the skill displayed in the construction and wording of the claims. The shorter and the more concise the language of the claims as a rule the better. It is the purpose of the present

chapter to make a few cardinal expositions from
personal experiences with inventors and research workers, as well as attorneys, in the hope
of broadening the horizon of the younger and
less experienced research student and inventor,
and to give the layman some idea of the charm
and of the profits, and on the other hand of the
disappointments and the pitfalls, of the inventive game in America.

American inventive genius ranges all through
a scale, from a very poor and ignorant type to
a well to do and highly educated and skilled
type.   Let me give you two selected personal
experiences from a long practice with both
types.   I will begin by choosing the poor ignorant type, a good case of which I encountered
during a recent visit to a small western town
where I was called into conference to see a new
invention.   I was in this little community on
engineering work in connection with a different
matter when it was learned that I was an engineer and supposed to be " wise " in matters
of research and invention, and I was asked if
I would not step around the corner and look at,
and give my opinion on, what was believed to
be a very promising invention.   I did so.   The
laboratory and experimental shop was dark and
disorderly, and the inventor very enthusiastic,
a typical characteristic, and a bit excited over
the visit from a city man, and he led the way

to the innermost shrine where stood the invention. The model was rather clever for economic production in its design and construction, but upon testing it out it would have failed woefully to function or operate as intended, and it only took a few moments to note that the entire principle was wrong. The patent had been secured by one of the patent quacks already mentioned. There was the eager inventor ever hopeful that his next model, if slightly modified, would work, and his friend (?), the local capitalist who had put up a few dollars for his half interest, or to be more correct and technical, his 51 per cent. It took but a glance to see, as stated, that the fundamental principle was wrong and very old, and that there were scores of patents already issued for substantially the same thing, and that his " no patent no fee " quack firm of attorneys had simply, as far as a patent was concerned, secured one narrow insignificant claim of some *seventy words,* but nevertheless with the red seal and the blue ribbon of the United States Patent Office. It was a difficult task to tell the inventor that there was nothing in his invention, and although it was explained to him that I was a member of the American Society of Mechanical Engineers, as well as a member of a University Faculty, which by the way meant practically nothing to him, he took my opinion with suspicion and

THOMAS ALVA EDISON
Electrician and Inventor

Born at Milan, Ohio, February 11th, 1847. Received some instruction from his mother; (Honorary Ph.D. Union College, 1878; D.Sc. Princeton University, 1915; LL.D. University of the State of New York, 1916).

At 12 years of age became newsboy on the Grand Trunk Railway; later learned telegraphy; worked as operator at various places in the U. S. and Canada; invented many telegraphic appliances, including automatic repeater, quadruplex telegraph, printing telegraph, etc. Established workshop at Newark, New Jersey, removing to Menlo Park, New Jersey, 1876, and later 1887 to West Orange, New Jersey.

Invented machine for quadruplex and sextuplex telegraphic transmission; the carbon telephone transmitter; the microtasimeter for detection of small changes in temperature; the megaphone, to magnify sound; the phonograph; the incandescent lamp and light system; the kinetoscope, the kinetograph, the kinetophone, telescribe, alkaline storage battery; since commencement of European War, 1914, designed, built and operated successfully several benzol plants; also two carbolic acid plants; also other chemical plants for making myrbane aniline oil, aniline salt, and paraphenylenediamine. Has received patents for more than 900 inventions.

Was made Chevalier, Officer, and afterwards Commander of Legion of Honor, by French Government; appointed 1903 Honorary Chief Consulting Engineer St. Louis Exposition, 1904. Awarded John Fritz Medal, 1908; Rathenau Medal. President Naval Consulting Board since July, 1915.

resentment as being either based upon incompetence or upon ulterior motives. The human side of this type of inventor is very hard to deal with, and for this very reason the problem of protecting him is all the more difficult. Here was a case, and there are thousands like it in every State in our Union, where all four of the elements of success were wrong. First, the inventor himself did not have the education and training to deal with the type of problem he had chosen; secondly, the laboratory and experimental shop were totally inadequate to perfect such a device, very much on the order of a blacksmith shop undertaking the making of scientific instruments; thirdly, the patent firm knew full well that it had robbed the man when it encouraged the taking out of a patent; and, fourthly, the inventor's business associate was in a strong strategic position to freeze the inventor out immediately if the invention proved to be of any value. The business associate drew me aside and said, "I put up two hundred and fifty dollars for experiments for a 51 per cent interest, and the money has been spent. If you think well of the invention I will put up another hundred dollars for another quarter interest." "Yes," I said, "when this is spent, you can then offer fifty dollars more for a further interest, and gradually absorb all of the equity in the invention." It was a pleasure for me, after I had secured the inventor's permission to express myself, to tell the capitalist that the entire principle was wrong, and when I left, the inventor's associate was endeavoring to get back the money he had advanced. It is an old and cunning game for a shrewd capitalist to acquire a half interest in an invention, for a definite sum, the money to be spent in developing and perfecting the invention, the capitalist knowing full well that the money advanced is not enough to reduce the invention to practice, and that a new deal with the inventor must be made before even the first working model is completed. An inventor ninety-nine times out of a hundred will, unconsciously and unintentionally, underestimate the funds required to perfect a device. It is usually a wise plan after carefully estimating the probable cost of developing a new invention as carefully as you can to multiply the figure by about five.

Let me give you another case, one of the other extreme. A college professor had written and retained me for my assistance in connection with an invention he had made, and I went to his city to examine the device. He knew the prior art in a thorough and scholarly manner, and his protection was skillfully provided by honest and competent attorneys. His patent was, therefore, basic and strong in thoughtfully drawn concise claims, but the instrument in its design was grotesque in the extreme, and impossible to look at without an irresistible desire to laugh. To think of making it economically in one thousand lots in a factory, would make anyone with a knowledge of machine shop practice hysterical. The model resembled a huge spider standing very high, with its back up like a cat's, and was complicated beyond words. But it worked, and moreover contained the germ of a great invention, and since has revolutionized an industry, but in its original shape it was not possible of practical manufacture. The original design required impossible castings, the most costly "milling" operations, "blind assembly," hand fitting and scientific adjustment of a most elaborate character. It had to be placed absolutely level and away from all vibration to work, and a skilled factory foreman would have thrown up his hands in horror at the thought of making the thing practically and commercially and in turning out finished instruments in quantity lots at *any* price. I told the inventor that the invention was a brilliant one; he knew this, of course, but he did not seem to appreciate that the design was utterly impossible. He did not distrust me, like the more ignorant fellow I have described. "I know," he said, "that the device requires some little modifications and that is why I wanted someone to help me in the matter." The design

was subsequently reduced to practice, a few
simple die castings replaced the impossible
sand core shapes and eliminated the milling,
a long suspension was replaced by a jeweled
movement with hair spring control, and a magnetic damping device eliminated the necessity
of levels and a base free of vibration, and today
the invention is a scientific and commercial
success.   I have taken two rather extreme
cases, but it will be appreciated that lying between them are many gradations.

One cannot make a survey of American invention by going into the workshops and homes
of inventors throughout the land without see-
ing evils of one kind or another at work, but it
is particularly pathetic to watch poor fellows
without the educational equipment, struggling
with problems far beyond their capabilities and
without the means of obtaining honest and
ethical advice.   A national society with a fund
to assist worthy inventors in America would
render one of the greatest and most valuable
services to the country.   In all of my studies,
academic and practical, in the laboratories of
universities as well as in the shops and factories of this country and Europe, few things
have impressed me as so urgent for development as more painstaking research for America
and a liberal endowment for assisting worthy
men with meritorious inventions.

APPENDIX

Problems Awaiting Solution

There is a famous saying, "Hitch your wagon to a star," and in conformity with the ambitious character and dignity of this well-known quotation, we will list first in our appendix some of the famous problems of the greater light, and of the first order of economic magnitude.

If we concede that physics and chemistry are the great underlying sciences which now interest us most, we will limit the list of problems awaiting solution to one or the other of these great fields of endeavor and reward.

Before actually listing the selected problems let me place before the reader the following question, which is in itself a problem, and let him try to decide which would be the greatest triumph of man, the one in physics in the unlocking of atomic energy, or the one in chemistry in the synthesis of food.

Let us take the great possibility in the domain of physics first, and I will quote from a letter from Professor Bergen Davis of Columbia University in reply to the author's request for great problems in physics awaiting solution.

" In the domain of pure physics, aside from any special problems, I think the whole matter might be summed up or summarized under one or two heads. The great problem in physics which includes all the lesser problems, since its solution would solve most of the lesser problems, is the constitution of matter, the construction of the atom which includes the nature of all radiation, or radiant energy and the nature of the medium in which these atoms are immersed and in which the radiation is propagated.

"As you know, progress is being made in experiments bearing on energy and the constitution of the atom and the nature of radiation. Many investigations are now being carried on tending to throw light on the Bohr model of the atom and the energy quantum which is found to control all processes of energy radiation now investigated."

Professor Davis has very concisely stated the problem and in a very comprehensive manner, and we may do well to try to appreciate just what the solution of this problem would mean.

" The new studies in radio-activity have taught us that every molecule of matter locks up among its whirling atoms and corpuscles a store of energy compared with which the energy of heat is but a bagatelle. It is estimated that a little pea-sized fragment of radium has energy enough in store, — could we but learn to use it, — to drive the largest steamship across the ocean, — taking the place of hundreds of tons of coal as now employed.

The mechanics of the future must learn how to unlock this treasure of the molecule; how to get at these atomic and corpuscular forces, the very existence of which was unknown to science until yesterday.

" The generation that has learned that secret will look back upon the fuel problems of our day somewhat as we regard the flint and steel and the open fire of the barbarian."

The boldness of this proposition may shock the ordinary reader, yet may we not ask if its solution would be one whit more wonderful than our accomplished mechanical flight, the wonders of X-Rays, or the wireless telegraph and telephone?

Let the reader try to fully appreciate what the solution of this problem of releasing atomic energy would mean to mankind from the economic point of view with all of its ramifications, and then let him try to fully appreciate what the solution of the following problem in chemistry would mean. Here is the problem just as majestic and just as alluring, a fit companion from every angle to the superb one in physics.

" The new synthetic chemistry sets no bounds to its ambitions. It has succeeded in manufacturing madder, indigo, and a multitude of minor compounds. It hopes some day to manufacture rubber, starch, sugar — even albumen itself, the very basis of life.

" Rubber is a relatively simple compound of hydrogen and carbon; starch and sugar are compounds of hydrogen, carbon, and oxygen; albumen has the same constituents, plus nitrogen.

" The raw materials for building up these substances are everywhere about us in abundance.

" A lump of coal, a glass of water, and a whiff of atmosphere contain all the nutritive elements, could we properly mix them, of a loaf of bread or of a beefsteak.

" And science will never rest content until it has learned how to make the combination. It is a long road to travel, even from the relatively advanced standpoint of today; but sooner or later science will surely travel it.

" And then who can imagine, who dare predict, the social and economic revolution that must follow?"

Which of these two problems is the most majestic? The keys to the solution of them both are lying everywhere about us, yet concealed from view. Who will scratch below the surface and see the glitter revealed of the golden key for the unlocking of either of these great secrets?

Among other possible triumphs in the problems in the domain of physics and chemistry are the following:

Electricity Direct from Carbon

Light without Heat

The Fixation of Nitrogen ·

Wireless Transmission of Power
The Perfect Storage Battery
Use of Wave Power of the Restless Sea
Use of the Sun's Radiant Energy
The Artificial Production of Rain
A New Fuel for Internal Combustion Engines
The Rotary Gas Engine
A New and Enduring Road Material.

Some of these problems appear to be purely physical and others appear to be purely chemical, while quite a number reach out into both fields, and the worker who hopes for success must possess a knowledge of the great underlying principles of both physics and chemistry.

The literature of the above listed subjects is fascinating and instructive, and the reader is advised to spend as much time as he can afford in reading the literature of these arts.

The following selected list of minor problems involves also, to a surprising degree, both physics and chemistry, and they are given here as of great promise to the research worker.

The author has been in correspondence with the foremost and ablest technologists in quest of problems, and here are some of the suggestions received for research.

Chemical and Physical Data

In my opinion, we are not lacking so much in ideas as to what needs solution as we are in *data* with which to tackle the problems which stare us in the face.   I mean the requisite chemical and physical data needed for the engineering solution of the many problems before us.

For instance: We need *data* of heat conductivity of metals and refractory substances between high and low temperatures.   This would enable us to more properly design furnace walls and utilize high resistivity materials.

We need *data* about heat emissivity of various materials at various temperatures.   This would enable us to determine how quickly they would heat up in a hot space and how quickly they would lose heat out in the open.

We need thermochemical data about the heat of formation of alloys — such as steel, bronze, etc. Very few of these are known.   They would enable us to determine the volatility of zinc from brass, for instance, with precision — and many other difficult problems.

We need *data* on the vapor tensions of the metals. This would enable us to size up losses by volatilization at different temperatures and under different circumstances.

We need *data* on latent heats of vaporization of the metals.   This would enable us to size up the heat losses in electric furnaces caused by volatilization of the products — such as Mn, Si, etc.

We need the *electric conductivity* of metals and re-refractory materials at high temperatures.   Very few of these are known.

We need *heats of formation* of many substances

and compounds not yet determined — such as FeS_2, mattes, and slags. The data on these are woefully deficient.

And so I could go on. We know how to use ten times the physical and chemical constants which we have. The trouble is that no one seems to realize that the trouble is just here — lack of fundamental data. Given these, we could solve many, many questions which are a standing challenge to metallurgists and chemists.

Joseph W. Richards, Bethlehem, Penn.

Synthetic Compounds

(1) Production of diamond in commercial quantity and good sized masses for use as abrasive, for cutting tools and bearings.

(2) The economic synthesis of sugar, fats and proteids, of a character suitable for food, from elementary substances.

Charles E. Munroe, Washington, D. C.

Problems in Physical Chemistry

(1) A catalyst for the reaction $CO + H_2O = CO_2 + H_2$ at low temperatures under 300 deg.

The calalyst must not be easily poisoned by the ordinary poisons in water gas.

(2) Solubility of H_2 and N_2 in water at various temperatures and at high pressures (50 to 100 atmospheres). Also work upon the effect of CO_2 on these solubilities.

(3) The mechanism of the absorption of CO

by cuprous and ammonia solutions and the effect of pressure and temperature on the reaction.

(4) Catalysts for synthesis of ammonia from nitrogen and hydrogen.

(5) Acceleration of reaction $NO + O_2 = NO_2$.

(6) Utilization of high tension electric currents to bring about more efficiently combination of nitrogen and oxygen, probably by ionization of the gases.

Colonel Alfred H. White and Captain Tour, U.S.A.

Chemical and Physical Data

The further study of the development of light without heat.

The combination of the higher thermal efficiency of the gas engine, with the efficiency of the steam turbine by combining the two in the form of a gas turbine.

The *energy* reactions in metallurgical work should receive more attention than they do. By studying these energy reactions, often largely involved in physical instead of chemical processes, greater economy might be possible. In the purification of zinc, for instance, by distillation, a reduction in atmospheric pressure, which becomes possible with electric furnaces, might reduce the energy required greatly.

A study of the vacuum furnace for refining. The vacuum furnace on a large scale becomes possible with some forms of electric furnaces, the resistance types as distinguished from the arc types.

The interchange of the atoms in carbohydrates to convert them from an indigestible to a digestible form. The fungi show us that this can be done.

The study of utilizing the work done by bacteria, as in the production of alcohol, the fixation of nitrogen, etc.

Energy from the indirect combustion of fuel, to evade the thermo-dynamic law which so greatly limits the steam engine. If, for instance, zinc were reduced by a thermal process and then used to generate current, this would be one way, but this particular way would not be practicable.

Extracting the heat from cold air for the heating of dwellings, as proposed by Sir Wm. Thomson over 50 years ago; it now becomes possible with the use of electric motors.

The fixation of nitrogen using liquid air.

The study of Nature's process in the fixation of nitrogen, which she used in the formation of the Chilean saltpetre, and reproducing this process artificially.

Carl Hering, Philadelphia, Pa.

Cost-recording Devices

(1) Complete cost-recording devices, especially for labor. I know of none that does the whole string of tricks, from the pressing of a button each time a worker changes his work, all the way down to the summing up of each workman's time (value) and the value of the time on each unit

for division of the bill of each customer, and make readily available the totals of departments. It would be no difficult matter to ring in the overhead and machine "times" (values of time) of presses, and perhaps even the floor space occupied by forms and type, etc.

(2) We have time-recorders that make records in response to the press of a button, but the records have to be transcribed. We have elapsed-time machines, but the men have to go some distance to get to them, and their results must be subsequently summed up. We have "Trautwine's Pay Register System" but that is not yet developed to the point where it can produce economically detailed costs for various customers.

(3) In the case of the street-car, at least, it should be quite practicable (now that we Philadelphians are being trained to a "pay as you leave car") to have distance recorders on each car. Each passenger, on entering, would be given a ticket with an initial charge of say two or three cents (to cover starting and stopping costs) and would then have his ticket handled like the time tickets in elapsed-time machines, except that each passenger's ticket would show, when he left the car, the value of the distance traveled (in addition to the initial charge).

John C. Trautwine 3d, Philadelphia, Penn.

Sound Producing Instruments

A telephone or phonograph is wanted that will clearly distinguish between "f" and "s" and

" m " and " n " and between " b," " d," and
" t." The fact that both the violin and the organ
have been left undisturbed for a century or so,
with a reverent " hands off " attitude, does not
prove that improvement is impossible.

In music, radically new methods of sound production should be sought and developed. Some
years ago some people in New York put together
a machine with revolving armatures, which sent
out electric waves, and these could be elaborately mixed and combined to reproduce known
instruments, or to create idealized tones.

There is also the " Coralcelo," in which piano
or similar strings are made to vibrate by electro-
magnets, each string being accorded a commutator of its own, which supplies the impulses
just when they ought to come.

John C. Trautwine 3d, Philadelphia, Penn.

Surface Contact Street Railroad System

We need a developed and perfected surface
contact system for electric traction in city streets,
allowing us to do away with the unsightly and
dangerous overhead trolley wire, without the inordinate expense of the unreliable underground
slot system.

The surface contact system has never been reduced to perfect performance, and there is a crying
need for the best engineering talent to design the
street railroad of the future.

There will be sooner or later an active campaign
against the menace of the overhead trolley, a con-

stant source of peril to the fire-fighters in such cities as Baltimore, Philadelphia, Boston, Providence, and a score of other large cities, in addition to frequent accidents to men and animals in the streets through falling wires.

This system has not yet been perfected and installed in the United States, but its ultimate development is certain.

C. E. Jenkins, Philadelphia, Penn.

New Insulator.

(a) A high voltage line insulator which is immune to puncture (will always flash over before it will puncture), and which cannot be damaged by the power arc following a flash over. This will probably involve research directed towards producing porcelain, or other ceramic material, capable of withstanding the sudden application of high temperatures, which will probably mean high tensile strength, high melting point and extremely low coefficient of expansion.

(b) A material of high dielectric strength and durability which can be made in large masses and can be machined.

(c) The direct formation of explosives, and of nitrogen compounds, by electrolytic action at comparatively low voltages; probably under extremely high physical pressures.

(d) A highly sensitive amplifier unaffected by external electrostatic and magnetic fields, and unaffected by mechanical vibration, which will *stay* in adjustment.

Ralph D. Mershon, New York, N. Y.

Uses for Glycerin and Phenol.

There are a number of subjects which we have not gone into very deeply, which are interesting, as, for instance, the enormous supplies of glycerin and phenol that were left on hand after the war and for which no uses have yet been found, with the result that both these important chemicals are away overproduced. Recent issues of Drug and Chemical Markets, published weekly by D. O. Haynes and Co., 3 Park Place, New York, contain several articles on the present condition of a number of important products, occasioned by the war. Certainly new uses for glycerin are much needed, and this is a good subject for research. I think the same thing is true of phenol and probably there are many other important products in the same condition.

Allerton S. Cushman, Washington, D. C.

Airplane Instruments.

For airplane navigation better instruments could be developed. The compass is far from satisfactory, with the gyroscope compass not yet developed in light enough form. It is very possible that the future steering of airplanes will be along wireless rather than magnetic lines with definite control between cities.

W. B. Stout, Washington, D. C.

Supercharging Engine.

The cylinder of the aeronautic engine takes in per cycle a cylinder full of air at substantially the atmospheric pressure about the carburetor. As the airplane ascends, the density of the air diminishes and there is, therefore, taken in per cycle a decreasing weight of air and hence a decreasing weight of oxygen. This reduces correspondingly the amount of fuel which can be burned per cycle and hence the power developed.

It results that, as the airplane ascends to high altitudes meeting air of decreasing density, the power falls off accordingly, and very nearly in proportion to the density.

To meet this difficulty means are desired for supplying to the engine or to the carburetor air at nearly a constant pressure. This implies some form of air compressor taking in air at reduced pressure and density and delivering to the engine air at normal or nearly normal atmospheric pressure and density. This problem has already been solved or approximately solved so far as merely compressing the air is concerned. It is primarily a problem of finding the *best* way of meeting the various limiting requirements regarding space, weight, reliability, etc.

Bulletin No. 3, U. S. Naval Consulting Board.

Two Cycle Engine.

If an engine operating on the two cycle program can be developed, with fuel economy and general reliability equal to that of the four cycle engine, the relation of weight to power should admit of substantial reduction.   This is a favorite field for inventors and a large number of designs have been submitted.   The field is still open.

Bulletin No. 3, U.S. Naval Consulting Board.

Ignition.

This is a most promising field for experimental investigation.   Owing to the fact that modern engines develop explosion pressures of from 400 to 600 pounds per square inch and a mean effective pressure of 120 to 135 pounds, the problem of spark plugs is a difficult one.

The insulation must be capable of withstanding the enormous temperatures developed, and the plug must not leak.   A slight leak past the insulation for a period of 30 seconds would cause complete failure of the plug.   The spark points of the plugs must be maintained at a sufficiently high temperature to prevent an accumulation of carbon on them, and yet their temperature must not be high enough to cause pre-ignition of the combustible charge.

This means that the spark points must be maintained within a critical temperature zone.

The chief trouble encountered with spark plugs up to date has been that at low engine power the temperature of the spark is so low that the points rapidly become carbonized and the plug is short circuited.   This carbonizing can be corrected by a better system of lubrication.

E. H. Sherbondy, Washington, D. C.

Materials for Airplane Construction.

For wing surface or covering, linen or cotton fabric is now in common or practically universal use.

Sheet metal or metal fabric has received some attention. The chief advantage would be non-inflammability and perhaps greater durability. No wing covering can be considered which is markedly heavier than present forms for the same strength. Present coverings weigh from 4 to 4.5 ounces per square yard and have a tensile strength per inch of width of 70 to 80 pounds.

Any proposed substitute form must also give a smooth and continuous surface comparable with present forms.

For the wing skeleton or frame, spruce and wood veneer are commonly employed. Broadly speaking, the frame is of wood construction of one design or another.

Steel or aluminum alloys are attracting attention and seem to offer possibilities.

Any form of construction in metal must meet sensibly the present relation between strength and weight. This means that the wing must be capable of sustaining up to the point of rupture a distributed load of not far from 100 pounds per square foot.

No one should undertake the development of such construction without expert advice in applied mechanics, experience in steel construction, and with large shop and fabricating facilities available.

W. F. Durand, Washington, D. C.

The following suggestions for research are taken from " Scientific and Industrial Research," as conducted by Professor Vladimar Karapetoff in the columns of the " Electrical World," and are reproduced here through the courtesy of the Editor of this valuable publication.

Mining Applications of Electricity.

Further development of explosion-proof motors for coal mines, suppression of arcing in mine locomotive controllers, electrically operated reciprocating drill, self-contained portable electric lamp for miners and wider use of electricity in cutting coal and in other operations.

A. I. E. E. Committee on the Use of Electricity in Mines.

Lightning.

A miniature laboratory arrangement imitating a charged cloud and a transmission line, to study the effects of direct and indirect lightning strokes.

Editorial Suggestion.

Camera for Rapid Successive Exposures.

A camera with 24 lenses has been developed that will make 24 successive images at a maximum rate of 500 per second. The focal-plane shutter consists of a long curtain, and when operating it uncovers each lens in succession. An electrically operated trigger for the setter starts it just before the phenomenon to be recorded begins.

Numerous investigations of arcs have been made by means of this camera, and have resulted in improvements in oil switches, circuit breakers, rotary converters, transformers, etc. The camera may also be readily adapted to the study of the spark gap discharges, insulator flash-overs, cable break downs, transformer coil displacements, busbar movements, gas engine operation, rifle and gun displacements, golf positions, etc.

Capt. Chester Lichtenberg, Washington, D.C.

Protective Devices.

In view of the proposed interconnection of transmission and distribution systems throughout the country, as a measure of economy and fuel saving, it is recommended that this subject be investigated thoroughly, particularly to determine what protective features are necessary in the lines for the purpose of insuring continuity of service and stability of operation. Among other subjects which might be investigated are the following:

1. Relays on generators, transformers, synchronous converters, etc.
2. Lightening arresters for transmission lines.
3. Preparation of definite recommendations regarding the standardization of relay nomenclature and rating of circuit breakers.
4. Detrimental effect of power reactors.

A. I. E. E. Protective Device Committee.

Batteries.

Some experiments seem to indicate that the electrolytic action in a lead battery is facilitated and made more complete in the presence of radio active salts, for example, radium barium sulphate. Further systematic experiments are desirable.

See a recent French patent issued to Mr. Thofehern, "Electrical World."

Magnets, Permanent Standard Test.

The committee on magnetic properties of the American Society for Testing Materials in its annual report 1918, recommends certain definitions of normal residual induction and of normal coercive force, and also proposes a standard test for material intended for permanent magnets. Those interested should perform these tests and investigate their accuracy. Universal applicability is desirable for practical purposes. This should be done before the society adopts these tests as standard.

Editorial Suggestion.

Lamp Sockets, Ventilated.

At the request of the Engineering Standard's Committee measurements have been made of the temperature in ventilated and unventilated sockets of lamps in lanterns of the open and inclosed types. There is considerable heating in the sockets owing to the conduction of heat from the bulbs, and it was found that the temperature in the leading in cables might rise to 140 degrees C., and that the existing arrangements for socket ventilation did not afford much relief.

C. C. Paterson, A. Kinnes, J. W. T. Walsh, and Dr. Norman Campbell; National Physical Laboratory, Teddington, England.

Telephone, Loud Speaking.

There is still a wide field for further improvements of loud speaking telephones and for a scientific study of the best conditions. The hot-cathode amplifier might easily prove to be a useful adjunct in such devices.

Editorial Suggestion.

Insulators.

Methods of testing faulty line insulators with lines in service.

D. D. Ewing, Purdue University.

Lightning.

More definite information regarding duration, frequency, current and voltage values and wave shapes of atmospheric lightning.

S. A. Stigant, Manchester, England.

Iron and Alloys.

An investigation of the effect of alloying substances on the magnetic and other properties of iron. Continuous work has been done for several years. The properties of electrolytic iron of great purity have been determined, and also the influence of various percentages of boron, silicon, aluminum, and nickel. Samples of iron having magnetic permeability far surpassing that reported by other investigators have been produced.

E. B. Paine, University of Illinois.

Flue-Gas Temperature Recorder.

Improvements are desired in electric or other thermometers for indicating and recording the temperature of flue-gases in modern power plants. The device should be capable of showing the average temperature over a large cross section, and the exposed parts must be so made that continuous immersion in hot flue-gases would not affect the accuracy of the readings. Instruments of this sort should be so arranged that they can be installed at any convenient distance between the sensitive instrument or the bulb, and the indicating and recording device without affecting their accuracy. They should be so arranged that checking and calibration can easily and accurately be done.

C. F. Hirshfeld, Detroit Edison Co.

Iron, Electrolytic.

The electrolytic production of iron on an industrial scale seems to have a bright future but it is accompanied by a polarization of electrodes. This is probably the only reason for which all iron has not been produced electrolytically, for a long time, like copper, which is electrolytically refined. It is of great interest to find out how the polarization varies with the nature of the electrolyte, its temperature, etc.

H. Le Chatelier, Paris, France.

Storage Batteries.

Determination of the charging current which will flow when a definite constant potential is applied to a storage cell under various conditions of state of charge, temperature, specific gravity of electrolyte, type of plate, age of plate, etc.

J. Lester Woodbridge, Electric Storage Battery Company, Philadelphia.

Fuses, Self-Resetting.

An inexpensive high tension magazine fuse for branches of rural transmission lines. The fuse should have, say, six wires, of which only one is inserted. Should it blow, the next wire should be placed automatically in the circuit. Should two or three fuses blow in succession, indicating a real trouble, an automatic catch should prevent the next wire from sliding into place.

Editorial Suggestion.

Transformer Operation at Temperature of Liquid Air.

It is desired to investigate economics that would result from the operation of a large power transformer at the temperature of liquid air or thereabouts. Such an arrangement is by no means unpractical, since liquid air could be circulated in pipes, or even perhaps be used as insulation. At such a temperature the resistance of copper is but a fraction of its value at ordinary operating temperatures, so that much higher copper current densities could be used, thus reducing the weight of copper and the length of the mean turn. The size of the core would consequently be reduced and, moreover, higher flux densities could be safely used.

Editorial Suggestion.

Thermo-Electricity. Possibility of Refrigeration.

A theoretical investigation is being made into the efficiency of a refrigeration process based on the Peltier effect. It is well known that when a current passes through the junction of two metals a reversible heat phenomenon takes place. For example, when the current flows from antimony to bismuth, heat is produced at the surface of contact, while heat is absorbed when the current flows in the opposite direction. Thus such a junction may be made to act as a refrigerator and in a familiar experiment ice is actually formed around the junction by placing it in cold water. The purpose of the present investigation is to deduce the most favorable conditions of operation and to determine the highest attainable efficiency on the basis of some late research into the Peltier effect.

A. W. H. Griepe, New York City.

Air Washers for Large Turbo-Generators.

In many cases the distance between spray particles is equal to hundreds of diameters of each dust particle, even with extremely fine sprays in the densest spray washers now built. A thorough realization of this condition will make it apparent that with density of spray alone, no matter how great, one cannot hope to produce an efficient washer, although it will help.

On the other hand, the method of directing the spray with respect to the path of the air is of first importance, and the future successful washer will probably be built with this consideration in view.

C. B. Humphrey, American Spray Company, New York.

Ammeter with Multiple Shunts.

There is a high-grade laboratory-type direct-current ammeter of foreign make in which external shunts of different range are introduced by simply turning a handle. In so far as the writer is aware no such instrument is made in this country, and it would be a great convenience for research and testing purposes if one were developed and marketed.

William L. DeBaufre, U. S. Naval Engineering Experiment Station, Annapolis, Md.

Interruptions in Service; Automatic Restoration.

When an accidental short circuit or an arc occurs in a power network and line switches begin to open feeders, the operator has a number of things to do quickly and in a definite succession. In order (a) to prevent confusion, (b) to restore the service in a minimum possible time and (c) to reduce undue stresses on the equipment, it is desirable to have an automatic emergency device which would perform certain duties ahead of the human operator as soon as the conditions became abnormal. Such a device may consist of a controller or a dial with various contacts, the shaft being driven by a small motor. As soon as trouble occurs a relay starts the motor and the controller trips generator field switches, closes them again after a few seconds, introduces some resistance into the voltage regulator circuit, and performs such other operations as are necessary. A simple device of this kind has been described by F. E. Ricketts in the A. I. E. E. Proceedings of 1916, page 931, and a further development is very much desired, to take care of more complicated cases of interruptions.

Editorial Suggestion.

Lightning Arrester.

I hope to see an arrester, of the type of the oxide film or the aluminum cell, which has no spark gap, but is permanently shunted across the circuit and is capable of taking care not only of over-voltages but equally well of steep wave fronts and high-frequency oscillations, even if of lower than the circuit voltage. Such an arrester would give universal protection.

C. P. Steinmetz, A. I. E. E. Proceedings, 1918, p. 560.

Solar Energy.

Dr. Steinmetz has figured out that if all the potential water powers of the country were developed and every raindrop used it would not supply even our present energy demand. On the other hand, if only a small fraction of the solar radiation could be collected and used, it would be many times all the potential energy of coal and water.

Hence he concludes that solar radiation may be an important source of energy for the future (A. I. E. E. Proceedings, 1918, p. 597). Here is a great problem for the physicist and for the engineer, one worthy of endowed research for many years, because even a moderate success and an inefficient utilization of solar energy may be of inestimable economic value.

Editorial Suggestion.

Transmission Line, Experimental.

Transient phenomena, disturbances due to switching, deterioration of insulators, etc., could be conveniently studied on a full size experimental transmission line corresponding to an actual line, say, 100 miles (161 km.) long. Such an experimental line would be distinct from the usual "artificial" transmission lines used in laboratories, in that it should be of actual size, electrically speaking; that is, it must withstand service voltages up to 100 kv. and carry several hundred amperes per phase. Furthermore, the proposed line should be suitable for experiments on oscillations up to say 1,000,000 cycles per second, and therefore must have its resistance, reactance, and capacity strictly distributed and not concentrated at a number of points as in the usual artificial lines. For convenience in experimentation the whole line should be housed under roof — for example, in a long factory building — so that the spans would have to be reduced to a fraction of their actual length, while preserving the electrical constants of an actual line of this size. A beginning in this direction has been made by Professor L. Lombardi of Naples; see Elettrotecnica of Nv. 5, 1917.

Editorial Suggestion.

Insulators, Leakage Resistance.

Some measurements on surface resistivity of various materials have been published by the Bureau of Standards, in 1915, especially at 90 per cent air humidity. Among the materials that have the highest surface resistivity in damp air are paraffin, resin, and sulphur, while glass and porcelain are among the lowest. L. New has recently shown experimentally the great advantage of insulators provided with a paraffin creepage surface (Bulletin de la Société Internationale des Electriciens, Vol. 8, p. 83). The subject deserves serious attention on the part of insulator designers, especially with voltages at which the surface creepage and not the dielectric strength may be the determining factor.

Editorial Suggestion.

Permeability at Low Densities.

Very little information is available concerning the permeability of iron and of its alloys in the region of minimum permeability occurring at very low densities. Iron has a low permeability of the order of 100 at exceedingly low densities, and this permeability is nearly constant throughout a certain range. Within this range the hysteresis effect is exceedingly small or negligible. When an iron core is used with a coil and when magnetic densities are within the range considered, the iron-core magnet has the advantages of an air-core magnet, namely, constant inductance and zero core loss, but has an enormously greater inductance. Further data concerning iron and alloys within this range would be of considerable value in special cases.

R. W. Atkinson, Perth Amboy, N. J.

Synchronous Machines, Transient Reactance.

I should like to see some one investigate fully the influence of saturation on the transient reactance of, say, a turbo-alternator. We calculate the reactance of the winding and obtain results which are fairly accurate for normal values of current in the stator. But does this value hold with an excessively large current, such as obtained at the instant of short circuit? Owing to the saturation caused by the excessively large leakage fluxes, does not the winding behave as if it were located in a core of high reluctance? So far as I

NIKOLA TESLA

Electrician, Inventor of Polyphase Power Transmission

Born at Smiljam, Lika (Border Country of Austria-Hungary), 1857. Educated one year at elementary school, four years at Lower Realschule, Gospic, Lika, and three years at Higher Realschule, at Carlstadt, Croatia, graduated, 1873; student four years at Polytechnic School, Gratz, in mathematics, physics, and mechanics; afterwards two years in philosophical studies at the University of Prague, Bohemia; (Honorary M.A. Yale, 1894; LL.D. Columbia University, 1894; Sc.D. Vienna Polytechnic).

Began practical career at Buda Pest, Hungary, 1881 — invented a telephone repeater — and conceived idea of his rotating magnetic field; later engaged in various branches of engineering and manufacture.

Since 1884 resident of the United States, becoming naturalized citizen. Inventor system of arc lighting, 1886; Tesla Motor and system of Alternating-Current Power Transmission; Generators of High-Frequency Currents, and effects of these, 1890; 1891; Tesla Coil, or Transformer, 1891; investigations of high-frequency effects and phenomena, 1891 to 1893; system of wireless transmission of intelligence, 1893; system of transmission of Power Without Wires, 1897 to 1905; Art of "Telautomatics," 1898 to 1899.

Method and Apparatus for Magnifying feeble effects, 1901 to 1902; since 1903, chiefly engaged in development of his system of World Telegraphy and Telephony, and designing large plant for transmission of power without wires, to be erected at Niagara. His most important recent work is in a variety of machines, as reversible gas and steam turbines, pumps, blowers, air compressor, water turbines, mechanical transformers and transmitters of power, hot-air engines, etc.

have been able to check this up, I believe this effect is present in 25-cycle generators, which are normally worked at fairly high tooth and core densities.

R. B. Williamson, Milwaukee, Wis.

Contacts, Oxidation of.

It is very desirable to understand the limitations in the design of circuit breakers, contactors, switches, etc., caused by oxidation on contacts. There is no question that the circuit-breaker contacts will increase in temperature quite rapidly under certain conditions. It is questionable whether contactors would show the same effect. This may be due (a) to the contactors being small and the circuit breakers large, (b) to a difference in design which produces a different action on the contact, (c) to trouble caused by something entirely apart from oxidation. This problem could be handled experimentally in an ordinary laboratory if the investigation were confined to comparatively small values of current. It is a very important subject to understand, as it is the basis for the limiting temperatures on many forms of contacts.

H. D. James, Pittsburgh, Pa.

Fuses for Direct-Current Locomotives.

A fuse adapted for a 3500 volt direct-current circuit, which shall be small enough to be placed in a locomotive cab and reliable enough adequately to protect circuits whose normal current is from 5 amp. to 500 amp.

Captain Chester Lichtenberg, Washington, D. C.

Impedance, Mutual.

While this term, as applied to telephone circuits, has been defined in the A. I. E. E. Standardization Rules, it is desired that a general mathematical expression be worked out similar to the formula for ordinary impedance, to avoid confusion in applications.

Editorial Suggestion.

Instrument Transformers, Effect of Overloads.

It is a well known fact that the indicating errors of a current transformer are widely changed if its magnetic circuit is accidentally overloaded. This is due to polarization effects, which constitute a perfectly definite ferro-magnetic phenomenon and have been studied from a physical point of view. It would be of great interest to obtain quantitative data on actual instrument transformers, showing the changes in ratio and phase error after heavy short circuits. These errors, indeed, must be expected whenever the measured current drops suddenly from a higher value to a lower. Such data would enable one to develop some standard process of demagnetization and would help to settle some other equally important practical and theoretical questions.

Edy Velander, Massachusetts Institute of Technology, Boston.

Insulators, Leakage Resistance.

Some measurements on surface resistivity of various materials have been published by the Bureau of Standards, in 1915, especially at 90 per cent air humidity. Among the materials that have the highest surface resistivity in damp air are paraffin, resin and sulphur, while glass and porcelain are among the lowest. L. New has recently shown experimentally the great advantage of insulators provided with a paraffin creepage surface (Bulletin de la Société Internationale des Electriciens, Vol. 8, p. 83). The subject deserves serious attention on the part of insulator designers, especially with voltages at which the surface creepage and not the dielectric strength may be the determining factor.

Editorial Suggestion.

Permeability at Low Densities.

Very little information is available concerning the permeability occurring at very low densities. Iron has a low permeability of the order of 100 at exceedingly low densities, and this permeability is nearly constant throughout a certain range. Within this range the hysteresis effect is exceedingly small or negligible. When an iron core is used with a coil and when magnetic densities are within the range considered, the iron-core magnet has the advantages of an air-core magnet, namely constant inductance and zero core loss, but has an enormously greater inductance. Further data concerning iron and alloys within this range would be of considerable value in special cases.

R. W. Atkinson, Perth Amboy, N. J.

Synchronous Machines, Transient Reactance.

I should like to see some one investigate fully the influence of saturation on the transient reactance of say, a turbo-alternator. We calculate the reactance of the winding and obtain results which are fairly accurate for normal values of current in the stator. But does this value hold with an excessively large current, such as obtained in the instant of short circuit? Owing to the saturation caused by the excessively large leakage fluxes, does not the winding behave as if it were located in a core of high reluctance? So far as I have been able to check this up, I believe this effect is present in 25-cycle generators, which are normally worked at fairly high tooth and core densities.

R. B. Williamson, Milwaukee, Wis.

Telephone Lines, Capacity of.

When a section of a telephone line with the arrangement of wires under consideration is not available for capacity tests, measurements can readily be made by the use of a satisfactory model. The capacities per unit length remain the same if all the dimensions of width and height are reduced in the same proportion. Furthermore, the conductivity or the permittivity of the medium may be increased. One suggestion would be to place the model in a tank of electrolyte with the vertical dimensions corresponding to distances along the line. Some preliminary work of this sort was published by Dr. A. E. Kennelly many years ago, but considerable further study would be required to get the method into a form sufficiently accurate for our work, in which, in studying unbalances, we were interested in the small differences of relatively large capacities.

H. S. Osborne, American Telephone and Telegraph Company, New York.

Alternator, High Frequency, High Power.

A high frequency, high power induction type electric furnace has been successfully developed and would become of extensive use in electrometallurgy if a suitable source of power were available. High frequency is desired in order to do away with the iron core between the existing coil and the heated metal, which serves as a secondary of a transformer. Moreover, power-factor correction, which is essential with this type of furnace, can be readily accomplished by means of condensers, provided that the frequency is high enough.

An efficient alternator is needed of 500 K.W. to 1000 K.W. rating at 12,000 cycles to 20,000 cycles per second, one of reasonable weight and price.

Editorial Suggestion.

Field Distribution, Electrostatic or Magnetic with Two Media.

The following problem has recently arisen in connection with the discussion of some A. I. E. E. papers on electrostatic fields and insulators. Let a field of force be established between two electrodes of some arbitrary given shape in a homogeneous dielectric. Consider the space occupied by a tube of force of finite transverse dimensions, limited by a lateral surface and by paths of the electrodes; fill this space with a dielectric of different, say higher, permittivity. The question to determine is whether or not the field distribution is thereby affected, so that some outside lines of force will enter the new dielectric on a part of their length and then emerge again. If such be the case, then the former lateral surface is no more an envelope for lines of force, and the field distribution must be determined anew. In the design of some recent insulators the assumption seems to have been made that the substitution of porcelain for the air in part of the field would not affect the dielectric flux distribution in the remaining air, provided that the porcelain surfaces are shaped along former lines of force. If this be so, then local stresses and ionization can be reduced and the flash over point considerably raised. While the practical achievement achieved seems to be quite notable, the theoretical basis for it is still in doubt and requires a proof as to its validity, exact or approximate.

Lightning Arresters.   The Use of Condensers to Eliminate Surges.

It has been the practice in certain sections of Europe, especially in Switzerland, to use comparatively large electrostatic condensers connected between the line wires of a high tension transmission line and ground to carry high frequency, high potential surges and electric discharges to earth.   A condenser will carry current in proportion to the frequency of the impressed potential, and line surges are in general of the nature of high frequency discharges to earth.

It should therefore appear that the use of condensers would be of material value and would afford considerable protection.

V. L. Hollister, University of Nebraska, Lincoln. (While such condensers may be too expensive in the present state of the art for universal use, experiments on a small scale are recommended to determine their effectiveness for the purpose.   The recently developed oxide film arrester (A. I. E. E., 1918) may also contribute to the solution of the problem, although the practical experience with it at the present writing has been only limited.   The great advantage of a condenser is that it has no spark gap in series with it and is therefore instantly active with high frequency oscillations. — Editor.)

Separator, Magnetic.

There is need for powerful magnets or groups of magnets and corresponding auxiliary apparatus adapted to extract magnetic bodies from broken stone or metallic ores which are being mechanically transported for feeding large crushers. Small bodies of iron, such as drills, hammer heads, railway spikes, large bolts, and nuts, etc., are liable to cause a serious break in almost any type of crusher, and large numbers of such iron bolts get mixed with stone dug by steam shovels and carried on belt conveyors. The separation of such objects on a large scale has proved a very difficult problem, but one very important. Magnetic separators now on the market are intended for a different type of work and cannot satisfactorily perform this duty.

Percy H. Thomas, New York City.

Circuit-Breakers, Recorders of Abnormal Conditions for.

(a) An automatic inexpensive instrument is needed which might be attached to the circuits of larger power systems and which would record the amperes, the volts and the power factor of abnormal current rushes. The results would be of inestimable value in the study and determination of ratings of oil circuit breakers. (b) An automatic instrument for recording the stresses produced in the arcs, oil bath, and air chambers of oil circuit breakers when clearing circuits of abnormal current rushes. Such an instrument must be very sensitive and respond with a degree of quickness comparable with that of an oscillograph.

Captain Chester Lichtenberg, Washington, D. C.

Commutator Motors, Alternating-Current.

Besides the usual methods of speed control of single-phase and polyphase commutator motors, speed regulation may be brought about by varying the permeance of the magnetic circuit. One way of accomplishing this result is by superimposing direct-current excitation upon the field circuit of the machine (see Osnos, Elektrot. Zeits., 1918, p. 205). Other methods may be possible, and a general study of this problem is timely in connection with expected revival of electrification of steam railroads.

Fuses, High Tension.

A fuse adapted for 33,000 volts to 110,000 volt circuits and which will protect potential transformers is needed.

Captain Chester Lichtenberg, Washington, D. C.

Insulators, Study of Stresses.

One method that has been used for mapping out three-dimensional electrostatic fields within insulators consists in using paraffin with lycopodium powder. The desired stress is applied while paraffin is in the molten state, and the particles of lycopodium arrange themselves along the lines of force. The paraffin is allowed to solidify and the field is studied by making a cross section along any desired surface. This or a similar method would necessitate making a paraffin model of an insulator and applying an electric stress to it while it is in the molten state, but this difficulty may not be insurmountable.

Polyphase Systems, Signs of Vectors.

Some confusion exists as to the signs of voltages and currents in polyphase systems, and these signs seem to be fixed arbitrarily in each problem, so that the student gets no definite rule for a new case. For example, in a delta connected system the line voltages are usually considered positive in the order AB, BC, CA, forming a triangle. But if one transformer, say BC, be missing, the voltages in the resulting V-connected system are marked AB, and AC, changing the angle from 120 degrees to 60 degrees. Similarly, currents are marked on diagrams of connections with arrow heads to indicate the *positive* directions, and this is confusing because similar arrow heads are used in direct net works to indicate the actual directions of currents. What is needed is a definite notation and agreement for signs of vectors and also some suitable symbol to indicate alternating currents in conductors. This symbol must be such that the first Kirchhoff's law could be written with the proper signs and individual vectors, and at the same time it should not indicate the actual direction of currents at some one instant.

Power-Factor Meter, Indicating Minimum Value.

In many power supply contracts a clause is inserted penalizing the customer for a lower power factor. A power-factor meter is therefore needed in which the indicating hand can be originally set at unity or 100 per cent so that as the power-factor of the load drops below unity, the indicating hand will drop also. This hand should not rise again by itself even though the power factor became higher again, but an arrangement should be provided for resetting it at each monthly reading of the meter.

C. F. Mathes, Trinidad, Col.

Telephone Lines, Inductive Interference.

The possibility of danger to telephone employees and subscribers when service is established or interrupted on power lines paralleling the telephone lines may be worthy of investigation. A solution must be found which will enable a satisfactory operation of both power and telephone circuits in the same territory under all conditions of operation without disastrous interference.

The following list of problems has also been taken from the columns of "Electrical World" under the title of

Research in Progress or Completed.

The problems here listed are very stimulating and suggestive to invention, and are printed in the third issue of each month along with the *Suggestions for Research* in the columns of this enterprising and able magazine.

Research in Progress or Completed

Fuse Cut-Outs, Oil Immersed.

One cause of the uncertainty of operation of some large enclosed fuses designed for 2000 volts or more, lies in the porous filling used to suppress the arc. Under certain conditions of elevation of temperature this filling becomes a conductor, sometimes termed the "Nernst effect," and its effectiveness as an arc suppressing material is thereby destroyed. Exhaustive investigations have shown that most of the material suitable for use as a porous filling are affected in like manner. As a result a cut-out has been developed in which the fusible strip is placed under oil. The fuse link is under mechanical tension; on blowing, the ends are suddenly separated under the oil, and the arc is immediately extinguished without destructive disturbance. The homogeneity of the oil permits very close rating of the fuse. An important feature is the protection of the line-man in refusing the circuit, since many accidents and deaths have resulted from throwing in a new fuse on a short-circuited line. These devices have been developed for use at 2200 volts to 13,000 volts and with currents of one ampere to 3000 amperes.

L. W. Downes, Providence, Rhode Island.

Generator for Pulsating Currents.

A pulsating e.m.f. may be generated by means of a radical type homopolar machine. The disk should contain a number of slots the size of which should be equal to the cross sectional area of the pole pieces. The collecting brushes should be mounted in the same manner as used on all homopolar machines. The writer has built such a machine and has found it to give fair results. Such a machine should be of use in medical treatment where pulsating currents are used to a great extent.

Samuel D. Cohen, Brooklyn, N. Y.

Heat Transmission and Surface Roughness.

The effect of surface roughening on the heat transmitted from hot bodies to fluids flowing over them has further been studied, with some unexpected results. It was observed that with the degree of roughening obtained with the aid of a screw-cutting tool in the case of $1\frac{1}{8}$ in. (2.9 cm.) brass pipe, the heat transmission per unit of surface per degree difference of temperature between the metal and the water could be increased in the ratio of about two and a half to one for the same mean velocity of flow. The rule of Reynolds that the heat transmitted from a hot surface to the fluid moving over it is proportional to the frictional resistance between surface and fluid was thus practically confirmed.

Dr. Stanton and Miss D. Marshall, National Physical Laboratory, Teddington, England.

Oscillations, Linear-Sinusoidal Type.

The mathematical theory has been developed of an electric circuit which can act as a source of high frequency oscillations. A condenser is charged from a direct-current source and is discharged through a vacuum tube which contains a gas at low pressure and which allows the current to pass in one direction only. Suitable inductances are provided in the battery circuit and in the oscillating circuit. With this arrangement the voltage across the condenser varies practically as a linear function of the time during part of a complete oscillation and varies according to the sine law for another part of the oscillation. Such an oscillator is of particular advantage on ships where the source of electrical energy is a low potential direct current. The principal difficulty to overcome is to keep the discharge frequency constant at high frequencies. An apparently practical method for accomplishing this result has been theoretically developed by the writer and will be described later.

Henry G. Cordes, Bremerton, Wash.

Photometer, Integrating.

Satisfactory methods had to be devised for the photometry of gas-filled lamps. The ordinary step-by-step method is slow, particularly when the lamp cannot be rotated, and for most purposes a knowledge of the average candle power is all that is wanted. This can be obtained with the aid of the integrating photometer box suggested by Dr. Sumpner. It is a room rather than a box and should be spherical instead of cubical. The internal walls of the room are painted dull white;

the lamp under test, which may be a searchlight, is mounted or suspended in the box, and the beam passed out through a window in one of the walls, outside of which the photometer bench is mounted. In order to be able to examine the crater of an arc separately from the arc, the rays from the crater are reflected by mirrors through a second window so as to fall outside on the diaphragm disk of a second bench. This disk has a hole in the center and the light spot is, by a lens, magnified to cover the photometer disk. Light filters and standard vacuum lamps running at normal temperature are used in the measurements, but we are not satisfied with the arrangements, and these will be perfected as soon as conditions permit. Searchlight problems are also under examination.

C. C. Paterson, A. Kinnes, J. W. T. Walsh, and Dr. Norman Campbell, National Physical Laboratory, Teddington, England.

Standard Cells.

Some Western normal cells have been constructed and the laboratory standards of electromotive force have been compared with the standards of Japan, Dr. Yokoyama having brought three normal cells over to Teddington for this purpose. These cells, made in March, 1916, contain a ten per cent cadmium amalgam, and the mercuric sulphate was prepared electrolytically. They agreed with the National Physical Laboratory standard cells within seven, two, four parts (average four in a million), which is very satisfactory. The agreement of four other cells with a twelve and five tenths per cent amalgam, which were made by Dr. Shinidzu at Teddington in 1910, according to the instructions of the Laboratory (mercuric sulphate prepared by a chemical process), and which have remained at Teddington since, is not now quite so satisfactory. The preparation of the mercuric sulphate and the composition of the amalgam gave rise to long continued international researches before the war.

F. E. Smith, and H. C. Napier, National Physical Laboratory, Teddington, England.

Flux Distribution Between Segments of two Eccentric Cylinders.

This problem finds its application in the computation of the magnetic permeance of the air gap of an electric generator or motor, and also in electrostatic design; for example, in an umbrella-type spark gap. The problem has been solved by finding the proper form of conjugate functions which satisfy the boundary conditions. A similar problem for complete cylinders is solved in Webster's " Electricity and Magnetism."

James McMahon, Cornell University, Ithaca, N. Y.

Antennas, Electrical Oscillations in.

The mathematical theory of circuits having uniformly distributed electrical characteristics, such as cables, telephone lines and transmission lines, is applied in the oscillations in antennas and inductance coils. Methods have been worked out for determining the frequency of the natural oscillations of an antenna, analytically or graphically, when inductance coils or condensers are inserted in the lead-in. Expressions have been derived which permit the calculation of the effective resistance, inductance, and capacity of the antenna, and it has been shown that in so far as frequency or wave length computations are concerned, the simple formula applicable to ordinary circuits with lump constants gives very accurate results. Experimental methods have been developed for determining the effective and static or low frequency values of the antenna constants.

John M. Miller, Bureau of Standards, Washington, D. C.

Heater, Induction Type.

A new electric heater of the induction type has been developed which possesses a power factor as high as 95 per cent and whose humming noise, due to transformer action, may be kept quite low. The iron pipe through which the heated water flows forms the transformer core. The secondary winding consists of one turn which is a sheet of copper fitting snugly on the outside of the iron pipe. The primary winding consists of insulated copper wire wound around the secondary.

C. E. Magnusson, University of Washington, Seattle, Wash.

Hysteresis, Effect of Cross Magnetizing Fields Upon.

The effect of an alternating field applied at right angles to the direct field while the hysteresis curve was being traced has been investigated for steel specimens of varying degrees of hardness. The direct field reached a magnitude of 150 gausses, while an alternating field of a maximum field intensity equal to 80 gausses was applied in some cases. With soft specimens all traces of hysteresis disappeared; with very hard steel the width of the loop was reduced to less than one-tenth of that of the original loop. For soft steel the magnetization curve with the transverse alternating field applied lies almost wholly outside and beneath the normal hysteresis loop. With hard specimens it lies within the normal loop, except near the top, where it passes outside and above it. It is to be observed that the actual magnetizing field at any instant is the vector sum of three fields at right angles, and hence in general it is greater than either component. When the alternating field is applied it is found with hard steel that the longitudinal component of the flux is greater than can be produced by the longitudinal field. This seems to indicate a rotational hysteresis or a tendency for a large flux to maintain its magnitude while it is forced to change its direction.

N. H. Williams, University of Michigan, Ann Arbor, Mich.

Instruments, (Indicating) Criterion of Performance.

The origin and nature of hysteresis losses in typical instruments and methods of evaluation have been investigated in detail. This method occupies a field distinct from that of the usual methods of calibration in that it affords a criterion as to the performance of the type rather than as to the errors of an individual instrument, which latter errors are inherently subject to variation of a more accidental character. The investigation will be published in full in the *Journal* of the Franklin Institute.

Frederick J. Schlink, Bureau of Standards, Washington, D. C.

Machinery, Direct-Current, Armature Design Data.

Analysis shows the armature output to be proportional to the produce of the cubical contents, speed, allowable specific electric loading, polar arc, etc. Also, for a given output, polar arc, etc., the armature capacity varies inversely as the cube root of the speed. About ten high-class direct-current dynamos of various sizes and makes from one K.W. to ten K.W. were tested with due regard to armature dimensions, accepting the name-plate ratings as reasonable, and the curves were drawn giving various factors. Other curves prepared from the data show armature length as a function of armature diameter and speed for two-pole and four-pole dynamos with seventy per cent polar arc. Still another family of curves shows allowable watts per square inch of cylindrical surface of armature as a function of capacity and speed. This work ought to be further extended and checked with a considerable number of the very latest machines with confirmed ratings and supplemented by data in terms of various grades and thicknesses of armature laminations in use.

C. R. Wylie, Detroit, Mich.

Permeability, Influence of Magnetic Treatment on.

An investigation on laminated ring specimens was made by the ballistic galvanometer method. The apparent permeability for a given field strength, plotted against the low logarithms of the number of reversals of the measuring field before observation of the galvanometer deflection, gives an "accommodation curve." This curve shows clearly whether the iron is polarized, or demagnetized, and if so whether completely or not, and even indicates any preceding treatment with a field strength *smaller* than that used in measuring. If the iron is polarized, the curve slopes down; if demagnetized it tends upwards toward an asymptote. After an incomplete demagnetization the curve has a maximum, which is reached at a higher number of reversals the more carefully the magnetization is carried out. This criterion has shown that 90 reversals are entirely insufficient for demagnetization. About 300,000 were necessary for a good magnetization of a certain sample. Alternating-current and direct-current demagnetization proves to be absolutely equivalent for laminated samples and commercial frequencies, alternating current being the only one practically useful.

Edy Velander, Massachusetts Institute of Technology, Boston, Mass.

Radio, Antenna Constants.

An accurate determination has been made of the equivalent and true antenna constants for long horizontal aerials. One set of formulas is a logical sequel of the ordinary transmission-line equation and Dr. Cohen's graphical procedure described in " Electrical World," Vol. 65, Number 5. The problem may be solved directly with the slide rule. The second new method employs an approximate solution, but the formulas give about the same results as those of the first method. In both procedures the quarter wave-length distribution is considered, and both are in agreement with the actual conditions. A table prepared from experimental data shows the usefulness of the investigation.

August Hund, Berkeley, Cal.

Rectifiers, Aluminum.

Two matters of interest have been investigated that have received scant attention in former publications on this subject, *viz.*, first, the production of voltages higher than those usually obtained and, second, the wave-form of the rectified current. Forty lead-aluminum cells were used, grouped with ten cells in series in place of each of the four elements of the Nodon valve arrangement. A rectified voltage having a maximum value of more than 3000 volts was thus obtained, the r.m.s. value being 2600 volts. The wave forms were determined by means of the oscillograph. The current curve for all loads lies entirely upon one side of the zero axis. When the load is non-inductive, the voltage also is unidirectional, but with an inductive load the voltage curve shows small negative values at the minimum points. By graphical differentiation of the current curve the e.m.f. due to self-induction may be determined. It is found that the alternates of this curve account satisfactorily for the difference between the voltages when the load is inductive and when it is non-inductive. Efforts to obtain currents with as little fluctuation as possible were made by putting inductance into the load circuit and a condenser in parallel with the load. In some cases it has been possible to reduce the fluctuations of the rectified current from its mean value to a trifle over one per cent.

N. H. Williams, and J. N. Cork, University of Michigan, Ann Arbor.

Conductivity, Thermal, of Various Materials.

The thermal conductivity of various materials used in certain manufacturing processes was determined by measuring directly the amount of heat that passed through a thickness of material between two equi-temperature surfaces and the temperature drop through the sample. A soapstone electric heater was used for the source of heat, while the cool surface was furnished by a reservoir with circulating water. The temperature drop was measured by means of small copper-constantan couples. Among the materials tested were hard rubber, fiber, different kinds of wood, plate glass, soapstone, sheet steel, graphite (solid and powdered), lamp-black, etc. One fact that was noticed in particular was the large increase in the transverse conductivity of a pack of iron sheets when the individual sheets are painted with asphalt.

T. S. Taylor, Pittsburg, Pa.

Conduits, Thermal Conductivity of.

It is a well known fact that the insulation in high-voltage cables remains good only up to a certain temperature, after which the leakage through the insulation becomes such as still further to heat the insulation and cause its ultimate breakdown. It was therefore thought that if one kind of conduit radiated heat more rapidly than another it would be best to use the type which possessed the best heat-radiating qualities. At the writer's suggestion, W. S. Wilder has made some tests at the University of Wisconsin, and the results seem to indicate that vitrified clay dissipates heat at a rate of about ten per cent faster than fiber. There may, therefore, be some real advantage in the use of vitrified-clay conduit instead of fiber conduit for transmission cables, because with a given size of cable a heavier load may be carried on it than would be possible if fiber ducts were used.

G. G. Post, Milwaukee, Wis., Electric Railway and Light Co.

Instruments, Indicating — Determinateness of Hysteresis.

Experiments have been performed to determine whether or not hysteresis determinations on non-integrating instruments are reproducible within themselves. The data obtained indicate that such determinations are reproducible to a high order of precision, and it becomes possible to extend the definite utilization of such determinations in testing and calibration, with the noteworthy improvement in the precision of results of actual use of instruments. Certain fundamental laws representing instrumental hysteresis and the relation of that hysteresis to the use and testing of instruments have been derived and set down, and it has been shown that a remarkable improvement in the reliability of instrument observations is obtainable by the simple expedient of operating the instrument only through definite cycles subsequent to suitable regularization. The results will be published by the Washington Academy of Sciences.

Frederick J. Schlink, Bureau of Standards, Washington, D. C.

Lamps, Mercury-Vapor, Quartz Type; Decrease
in Radiation with Usage.

The object of the investigation was (1) to devise
methods of determining quantitatively the decrease in intensity of emission with usage and
(2) to make preliminary measurements on radiant-
power life tests of quartz mercury-vapor lamps.
The measurements of the radiations from these
lamps were made by means of a thermo-pile, in
front of which was placed a 1 cm. cell of water to
absorb the infra-red rays of long wave-lengths
emitted by the electrodes. The variation in intensity of the ultra-violet rays was determined by
observing the variation in transmission of a yel-
low Noviol glass with usage of the lamp. It was
found that the intensity of the total radiation as
well as the ultra-violet component decreased to
about one half to one third of its initial value in
the course of 1000 to 1500 hours. During the
first 500 hours of usage no marked difference was
observed in percentage of ultra-violet emitted by
two commercial types of lamps. Data have been
obtained (1) on the variation of the total radiation
emitted by quartz mercury-vapor lamps with variation in energy input, (2) on the variation of the
intensity of the irradiation parallel with the axis
of the lamps, and (3) on the variation of the intensity of the total radiation with distance from
the lamps. Comparative data have been brought
together on the ultra-violet component in the radiations from the sun, from quartz mercury-vapor

lamps, and also from a carbon-arc lamp which is used in dye-fading tests.

W. W. Coblentz, M. B. Long, H. Kahler, Bureau of Standards, Washington, D. C.

Materials, Self-Luminous.

For war purposes a brief statement has been prepared of those properties of self-luminous materials and of those principles of vision which should be known by all concerned with the drawings of specifications for the illuminating of articles by means of self-luminous material. This information will later be published by the National Advisory Committee of Aeronautics. A limited mimeograph edition was issued August 10, 1918, under the title, "Notes and Recommendations regarding Specifications for the Illuminating of Articles by Means of Self-Luminous Materials Containing Radio-Active Excitants."

N. E. Dorsey, Bureau of Standards, Washington, D. C.

Safety Codes, Industrial.

Extensive work is being done on the formulation of standard safety codes for various industries. For this purpose information is being collected and arranged, tests are performed where necessary, and the existing codes are studied with the view to their unification. The work includes safety of elevators, head and eye protection, power-transmission machinery, and apparatus, explosives, etc. A number of conferences and public hearings will be held in which interested parties will be invited, such as representatives of the various industries concerned, federal bureaus, state industrial accident commissions, some public service commissions, state authorities which make rating laws for casualty insurance, municipal authorities, technical and engineering societies, manufacturers' associations, employees' representatives, casualty insurance companies, etc. The work is being conducted in connection with the Working Conditions Service of the Department of Labor. The work of this department comprises industrial health, labor administration and industrial safety.

M. G. Lloyd, Bureau of Standards, Washington, D. C.

X-Ray Work, Protective Materials for.

Attention is called to the necessity for testing all material that is to be used for X-Ray protection. Some of the lead substitutes that are offered to the public for such use are practically worthless. The values of the lead equivalent of typical commercial materials have been determined.

N. E. Dorsey, Bureau of Standards, Wash., D. C.

Aluminum, Solders for.

The use, serviceability, method of application, and composition of solders for aluminum have been investigated in the light of special tests made at the Bureau of Standards on commercial and other compositions of solders and also as a result of general experience with them. All soldered joints are subject to rapid corrosion and disintegration and are not recommended except where protection from corrosion is provided. Suitable compositions for solders are obtained by the use of tin with the addition of zinc, or both zinc and aluminum, within wide percentage limits.

Bureau of Standards, Wash., D. C.

Anemometer, Hot Wire, Drop-of-Potential Type.

In this instrument the average velocity of flow of a gas is measured over a length of from 1 mm. to 3 mm. Two small 0.002 in. (0.05 mm.) platinum wires are attached about 2 mm. apart near the middle of the 0.007 in. (0.18 mm.) platinum heating wire. In calibrating and using it the current is measured that is required to maintain a certain potential drop — say 60 millivolts — between the two potential leads. A good portable potentiometer is sufficient for measuring the potential drop, while the current can be measured quite satisfactorily by a good ammeter of proper range.

T. S. Taylor, Westinghouse Research Laboratories, East Pittsburg, Pa.

Bearings, Spring-Thrust.

On larger bearings it is very difficult to establish and to maintain bearing surfaces fitting the journal within the limits of the thickness of the oil firm. If this is not done, the metals will touch and the friction will greatly increase. In the new bearings the surfaces are made of this flexible member supported in such a way that they can yield if overloaded over any small area. The usual support is by helical springs. The idea is to provide a bearing surface which is so yielding, flexible and elastic that it may conform to the rotating surface without creating at any point a unit pressure sufficient to destroy the oil film.

H. G. Reist, Schenectady, N. Y.

Conductors, Aerial, Wind Pressure on.

In connection with the preparation of the Electrical Safety Code, experiments have been made upon the shielding effect of several conductors with different directions of the wind. A tunnel was used in which the air velocity was controlled at will and the lateral pressure upon the conductors accurately determined. It has been found that the shielding effect of one conductor upon the other depends essentially upon the angle between the direction of the wind and the plane of the conductors. The shielding effect fell off rapidly as this angle was increased. No definite results could be accomplished in the open air.

M. G. Lloyd, Bureau of Standards, Wash., D. C.

Ignition Devices, Calorimetric Study of Spark.

Temperature curves were obtained which varied with the kind of thermometer used and with its position in the calorimeter. The pressure curves varied with the size and length of the pressure tubes. However, the same conditions were maintained in all the tests, and if the type of calorimeter used proves to be of practical value, it is proposed to work up specifications so that comparative results could be obtained anywhere by using common cheap supplies. It is interesting to note that the magneto giving the highest temperature curve does not necessarily give the highest pressure and vice versa. There seems to be some work to be done here.

F. W. Springer, University of Minnesota, Minn.

Illumination, the Measurement of Reflection and Transmission Factors.

A method has been developed for measuring the reflection and transmission of various light-diffusing media. The illuminating surface is a hemisphere of translucent glass inside a white-lined box. The material to be investigated is placed on a diametral plate and its brightness determined at definite angles by means of a photometer. This method is based on the principle involved in the Nutting absolute reflectometer, namely, two definite planes, one of which is opaque and receives all its illumination from the other. The relative brightness of the two planes measured with a comparison photometer is the absolute mean reflecting power of the opaque surface. Data have been obtained on ribbed and frosted glass. Numerous methods for investigating the optical properties of partly diffusing media were reviewed by the 1915 committeee on glare in the *Transactions* of the Illuminating Engineering Society, pages 353 to 378, July, 1915.

M. Luckiesh, Nela Park, Cleveland, O.

Inductance Coils, Electrical Oscillations in.

Inductance coils may be treated from the standpoint of the theory of the distributed inductance and capacity. Expressions have been derived for the reactance of a coil at any frequency and for the natural oscillations of a circuit of coil and condenser. It has also been shown that, in so far as the frequency of oscillation is concerned, an inductance coil with distributed characteristics is equivalent to a pure inductance of constant value with a constant capacity across its terminals. Excepting for skin effect, this pure inductance would be the same as the low-frequency inductance of the coil. This explains the fact which has been frequently observed experimentally, in particular for single-layer solenoids.

John M. Miller, Bureau of Standards, Washington, D. C.

Machinery, Electrical, Separation of Losses.

The machine under test is run idle as a motor at a constant speed, with various voltages impressed across the armature, the watts input to the armature being measured. In the case of a direct-current machine, the excitation and the voltage are changed simultaneously so as to maintain constant speed. With a synchronous machine it is desirable to maintain approximately unity power factor.

With induction machines the method is the usual idle running saturation current, the voltage being varied and the frequency kept constant. Volts are plotted as abscissas and the power input to the armature as ordinates. Assuming the curve to be a general parabolic one, the exponent of the parabola is computed and then extrapolated to the axis of ordinates; that is, to the voltage zero. The point so obtained on the axis of ordinates gives the value of the friction and windage loss. The remainder represents the core loss. The method will be described in detail in the A. I. E. E. *Proceedings*.

C. J. Fechheimer, Pittsburg, Pa.

Alternating Currents, Small, Measurement of.

Small alternating currents were successfully measured by means of a Rayleigh acoustic resonator. The resonator consisted of a brass cylinder closed at one end by a telephone receiver and open at the other end through a small tube in which a Rayleigh disk was suspended by a quartz fiber. Alternating currents sent through the telephone receiver set up vibrations of the air in the cylinder that caused the disk to rotate, the amount of rotation being noted by the deflection of a beam of light reflected from the disk. A 110-volt, 60-cycle alternating current gave readable deflections for currents of the magnitude of 1×10^{-5} amp. Later experiments indicated a greater sensibility.

F. R. Watson, University of Illinois, Urbana, Ill.

Aluminum and its Light Alloys.

All available information and bibliography concerning the physical and mechanical properties of aluminum and its light alloys have been collected and summarized. Commercial alloys have been investigated and compared. The corrosion and disintegration of aluminum and its alloys have also been considered. This information will shortly appear as a special circular.

Bureau of Standards, Washington, D. C.

Cables, Buried, Heating of.

A number of tests are being conducted on bitumen-insulated cables laid in stoneware troughs, lined with bitumen, as used for the low-tension supply of the Liverpool Corporation. The tests have been continued for a period covering an entire year, records of earth temperatures have been obtained, and the cables tested at a number of different current densities. This work is being conducted in connection with the research committee of the Institution of Electrical Engineers.

E. W. Marchant, University of Liverpool, England. [There should be such a research committee in the A. I. E. E. — Editor.]

Circuit Breaker Using Non-Inflammable Liquid.

This circuit breaker, for voltages up to 70,000 and for currents up to 150 amp., has been developed to obviate the shortcomings of oil circuit breakers, namely, their high cost, large space needed, the blowing out of the oil on heavy short-circuits and fire risk. The circuit breaker has been designed along the lines of the well-known carbon-tetrachloride fuse, except that the liquid used has a much higher boiling point because the circuit breaker cannot be hermetically sealed. The device consists of a vertical Bakelite tube, at the lower end of which is the stationary contact. The movable contact is at the end of a spring-actuated operating rod, and the current is conveyed by flexible copper connections. The tube is filled with a non-inflammable fire-extinguishing liquid, and a funnel-shaped arrangement on the movable contact forces a powerful stream of liquid upon the arc. A latch holds the breaker in the closed position and is released by pulling on a cord. An overload or reverse power relay may be attached to the switch to make it trip automatically

N. J. Conrad, Chicago.

Colorimetry of Nearly White Surfaces.

By means of multiple reflection between two surfaces of the color to be analyzed, a greatly enhanced departure from white in the normal color of the surface has been obtained. This enhanced color is compared with light from the same illuminant mixed in a known proportion with light of a pure spectral hue. Thus the dominant hue and percentage of white of the light reflected from the nearly white surface are determined.

A. H. Pfund, Johns Hopkins University, Baltimore, Md.

Magnet Steels.

An investigation has been undertaken of a number of alloys intended to be used in connection with the construction of permanent magnets. The alloys have been subjected to special heat treatment at the Hadfield works in Sheffield, and the magnetic testing is being carried on in this laboratory.

E. W. Marchant, University of Liverpool, England.

Neon Spectrum Measurements of Wave-Lengths.

The lines in the neon spectrum are very sharp, a quality which recommends this gas as a standard light source wherever the lines have sufficient strength. The ultra-violet group between 3369A* and 3520A may be used for standards, and there are a few good infra-red lines, but the strength and distribution of the lines in the region 5852A to 7438A make the neon spectrum particularly useful as a comparison in this region. The wave-lengths of fifty-five lines in the region 3369A to 8495A in the neon spectrum have been measured by means of the interferometer. One hundred and eighty-nine faint lines in the visible and infra-red neon spectrum (5343A to 8783A) have been measured by means of a concave grating.

K. Burns, W. F. Meggers and P. W. Merrill, Bureau of Standards, Washington, D. C.

[Neon is a gas which has some promise of practical use for illumination purposes in electric lamps of the vacuum-tube type. Lamps of this type are in an experimental stage and have been shown on one or two occasions. — Editor.]

Transformations, Electric, Possible with Stationary Apparatus.

A mathematical investigation has been made of inherent limitations of current and voltage transformations possible by means of a network constituted of self and mutual inductors, resistors and condensers. Expressions have been derived for electrostatic and electromagnetic energies, Joulean heat dissipation and power, in complex quantities. The purely imaginary part of the expression for power in a static network is shown to be equal to $2\,\omega$ times the difference between the mean electromagnetic energy and mean electrostatic energy, where $\omega = 2\,\pi\,f$. Use is made of this new principle in considering the problems of power-factor correction and phase splitting. In general, for phase transformation by static apparatus both magnetic and electrostatic storage of energy are necessary, and it has been shown how the mini-

CPSIA information can be obtained
at www.ICGtesting.com
Printed in the USA
BVHW071552100920
588449BV00007B/158

9 780548 925973